The Book of the Caves
Volume 1

The Golden Ring

A Practical Path to Inner Alchemy and Magic

Academy for Hermetic Arts and Sciences

Ina Cüsters-van Bergen

First edition published by the Academy for Hermetic Arts and Sciences 2025
CCProof ID 67ac6c47b57a8
ISBN 9789083585901

Grachtstraat 43
6305 AM Schin op Geul
The Netherlands

Visit our website;
www.hermeticartsandsciences.org

Contents

Introduction to the Book of the Caves

§ 1. Welcome

Welcome to my meditations on the Tarot deck *The Book of the Caves.* My name is Ina Custers-van Bergen. I am the director of studies at the Academy of Hermetic Arts and Sciences. I am the author, among them *The Temple of High Magic* and *The Mystery of the Sea.* I am a meditation trainer with over 35 years of experience in the Hermetic Mystery Tradition.

My mission is to help individuals achieve higher consciousness through transformative practices. As the head of the Academy for Hermetic Arts and Sciences I develop methods for students around the world to deepen their spiritual journeys.

In the course of my career I have authored more than 70 workbooks focused on meditation, ritual and the development of inner wisdom. In this book I offer a thoughtful introduction for those who are curious about the path of higher consciousness, and I will offer a glimpse into the practices and principles of working within an order. Whether you are beginning your spiritual journey or seeking to deepen your understanding, this book offers invaluable resources for those who want to practice the transformative powers of the Tarot, when used in meditation and ritual.

§ 2. The Mystery around the Corner

My journey with the Tarot cards started as a teenager. I went to Amsterdam to discover the wild world out there. I visited trendy places like the Kosmos. There, I bought my first pack of cards. I fell in love with the Tarot and never abandoned it. I have been admiring the beauty and the depth of their symbolism ever since.

At first, I used the cards to find answers to obvious questions about love and money issues: questions that are important to people in their daily lives. But something in the cards triggered me to dig deeper. A mystery appeared to be hidden just around the corner. I tried to find out what it was and discovered that the cards opened the way to even greater mysteries. I have worked with the cards since I was 17, and I am still learning from them. The Tarot gives access to the Matrix of Life.

§ 3. Doorways to the Inner Planes

I used the cards to find answers to questions about myself and situations that puzzled me. After thorough study and intense meditation, new and hidden depths started to surface. The cards became doorways to the Inner Planes. I discovered that, when working with a card, the Trump triggers new insights into events that are happening in my life. And when I followed their advice, situations started to change magically and I started to grow spiritually and as a person. I contacted energies that called themselves Inner Plane Teachers, guides on the highways towards the Higher Mind. My real adventure had now begun!

§ 4. Magical tools

The Tarot answers questions in an unexpected way. It does not use the rational mind. The Tarot is an ancient 'search engine' that enables you to delve deep into your subconscious mind and unlock hidden wisdom.

Excited by my experiences, I started to investigate the relationship between the Tarot and the Hermetic Kabbalah and I began to work magically with the cards. I experimented with them in combination with classical Astrology and ancient Mythologies.

The outcome of my research is so spectacular that I want to share my results with other people. So, I decided to draw my own deck of cards and call it *The Book of the Caves*. The name of this deck derives from Plato's allegory of the cave, in which Plato describes a world where people are chained to the wall of a cave. The only thing they see are the shadows cast on the wall. One of the prisoners manages to escape from the cave to the world outside and discovers that the shadow is caused by the light of the sun hitting an object. He returns to the prisoners. He tries to tell them about an unknown and extremely beautiful world outside of the cave. They do not believe him and dare not break the chains of their imprisonment because it is the only reality they understand.

§ 5. The Antique Worldview and the Caves of Consciousness

In antiquity, sages and priests compared different states of consciousness with caves. We find this concept in the famous Egyptian underworld books such as the *Book of the Gates*.

Every cave is a magical environment and has its own rules. We are all experiencing our reality in such a cave of consciousness. You can stay inside one, you can travel through it and also journey from Cave to Cave. Whenever you are in such a Cave, the events you experience follow a set structure, because every cave is aligned to the Matrix of Events of the Cosmos. Every Cave symbolizes an energy pattern that consists of complexes of ideas and ... every Cave preserves a magical secret that will transform your worldview and help you to rise above the issues that keep you in chains here and now.

Every Cave is like an empty stage of a theater play; the décor is prepared. The play starts when the actors take their places on the stage. By desire people are magnetically pulled into a particular 'theatre play' – an area of life – and are confronted with the challenges this particular area of life wants them to solve. Only when they see through the illusion of that particular Cave, they can free themselves from the shackles. If they try to escape too soon, life will mold a new version of the same play and the challenge unfolds once more.

Journeying through the Caves will teach you that your material environment is an illusion and that you can change your reality by changing the presumptions of the reality you live in. When you change the Cave – the pattern of your conscious awareness - old wounds can surface and a method for healing will come forth from your Inner Self. If you follow that path of transformation, the concepts that you hold 'true', including your physical circumstances, will change. This process is called magic. Magic can free you from the chains of the illusions that keep you imprisoned in your current situation. In becoming aware of these illusions, you stand a chance to free yourself from the chains that keep you in place and grow towards your true destiny.

The Tarot describes these 'Caves of Consciousness' in symbolic language. Symbolic because, although the events you go through are your personal experiences, the patterns they follow are transpersonal. This means that certain constellations of social interactions and human behavior are archetypical and follow natural laws, independent of the people involved.

Our modern Tarot deck has a history that goes back to unknown sources. But the essence of the deck contains parts that remind us strongly of the ancient Egyptian Underworld literature; the ancient Egyptian *Book of the Gates* is one of the famous books that explains to us how the Essence of the Sun travels through the Twelve Hours of the Night. Especially the *Book of the Transformations of Ra* is of interest in this context. The Sun sinks below the Western Horizon in the evening and makes a spectacular journey through the secret *Caves of the Duat*, in order to renew itself and become reborn the next day. In every phase of the Underworld Journey, the Sun God Ra needs to transform himself to get access to the next phase of the Journey through a magical parallel reality of the subconscious mind; the Otherworld. The Sun is a metaphor for our conscious mind, and it travels through the deep and mysterious world of the subconscious mind. It is a dangerous journey. On its road, the Sun meets Gods and helpful spirits, as well as enemies and dangerous entities that dwell in those Caves. Working with this Tarot deck enables you to make a similar journey through the 'Dangerous Waters of your Underworld' in a safe and harmonious way. In this way, the *Book of the Caves* is a modern version of an ancient technique you can use to improve your life, solve personal issues and walk between the worlds.

The symbols connected to each card are the keys to understanding the transpersonal patterns of that specific Cave, a limited world of consciousness with its own set of natural laws. When you know the laws, you can implement changes or even leave a Cave.

§ 6. Modus Operandi

In this book you find meditations about the great arcana cards that are connected to the Zodiac. For each card I have written a meditation to enable you to experience the Cave and to understand the symbolism that belongs to the various Caves. The main character of these meditations is Heru. Heru is a neutral name, a metaphor for your Inner Flame. This is the reason why I do not call Heru 'he' or 'she', but 'it'. Heru's name derives from the Egyptian god Horus. Heru means 'Light'. Heru is the Soul Flame which incarnates in a physical body and descends to Earth. Contrary to Christian belief, for example, we do not call this 'The Fall', but 'The Descent'. Our World of Matter is a sacred place and humanity's spiritual job is to improve this world. In this sense is Heru's mission is to become the 'Rescuer of Matter'.

The Golden Ring will be followed by a second book called:

- *Teachings from the Hidden Room, Conversation between the Soul and the Planetary Spirits.*

That book will deal with the Great Arcana cards that are connected to Alchemical Transformation processes, and the Planetary Cards.

After that book, four books about *The Enchanted Lands* – will come out, each one covering one season of the year from the perspective of the Minor Arcana cards:

- ➢ *The Enchanting Spring of Gorias: Awaken your life force with the Tarot's Minor Arcana,*

- ➢ *The Spellbinding Summer of Findias: Ignite your Passion and Power with the Tarot's Minor Arcana.*

- *The Otherworldly Autumn of Murias: Harvesting Wisdom and Transformation through the Tarot's Minor Arcana,*
- And: *The Magical Winter of Falias: Revealing Wonder, Beauty and Mystery through the Tarot's Minor Arcana.*
- The book: *The Crowns of Wisdom: Beyond the Veil of the Known through the Tarot's Royal Court* will follow later, this book contains a mystery...

Every book takes you through a module of the *Book of the Caves*. All meditation journeys are connected to the Hermetic Kabbala, classical Astrology and Mythology. The Hermetic Mysteries influenced a lot of cultures throughout history.

In all these cultures fragmented pieces of the Ancient Wisdom Tradition are hidden. Thus, the Hermetic Mysteries can be compared to a broken mirror, where all the pieces have to be gathered and put together again like a gigantic puzzle. This is how I developed the Tarot *The Book of the Caves*: from the many pieces of the puzzle, digging into the rich Western Mystery Tradition. From all the pieces of the puzzle I built a frame story and inserted some archetypical characters, to tell the story of Heru on the quest to Inner Wisdom. In every meditation journey, I will explain the energetic keys of the Tarot cards involved in the form of a story, so that you get an easy access to the inner energy of the cards and their transformative powers.

The guided meditations of this book are not designed to be stories, but rather tools – they train your mind and spirit in accessing deeper states of consciousness. They are not meant to entertain or distract you, but to guide you inward, to enable true growth, insight and healing to take place. Each meditation offers a mental technique, a pathway to help you unlock higher levels of awareness and will connect you deeper with your truest self.

Meditation is not an escape, but a mental training that teaches you to look inside, to awaken, and to create methods to explore the depths of your being. Through thorough meditation training, you will develop the ability to transcend your ordinary thoughts and worries, heal your wounds, and gradually develop full control over your mind, allowing you to access a deeper and more expansive sense of awareness, as well as find better solutions for the problems of everyday life.

My personal journey with the Tarot has changed my worldview and my understanding of the nature of reality. I want to share this beautiful, life-changing magical system by offering *The Book of the Caves* to you. It will open the doors to your inner riches and wisdom. Follow me into *The Book of the Caves*. It is a world of mysteries. The Caves are the deep layers of your subconscious mind. The scenes in the Caves will manifest in your daily life as experiences that bring new and deeper realizations of your talents and unlock new opportunities for growth.

These meditations form a curriculum in themselves and can also be combined with the other teaching programs of the Academy for Hermetic Arts and Sciences. These include The Online Journey, The Inner Journey, The Dragon's Journey, The Initiate's Journey,

The Adept's Journey, and The Egyptian Journey, as well as workshops, where theory, meditation training, and ritual are practiced as a group.

The first chapter of this book resembles the first story in the book *The Descent*. However, I made some changes that will make it possible for you to enter a deeper level of the story and to identify even more with the Child of Light, Heru. In this way, you will be able to continue the adventures of Heru after you have landed in the Enchanted Land.

Dedication to the Phoenix

The first-born son of Osiris

In the country called Self-luminous Bliss there lives a Spirit named Total Vision. Having no chair on which to sit, It creates a Throne of Water in the midst of the Cosmic Ocean. Having no clothes to wear, It weaves a Mantle from the Blackness of the Night. Having no food to eat, It sows its Essence into the Bottomless Ocean in the form of an Egg. When the egg is ready, it breaks into four pieces. In this way It plants the Four Elements for itself to feed on.

Longing to reunite with the Source, the Four create the Fifth: a huge dragon called Miraculous Inspiration starts to climb upwards: longing to become one with the Beloved. Looking upwards She falls in love with the Two Eyes.

She expresses her Glory, rises in Victory and grows in Beauty in her desire to unite herself with the Two Lights that show her the way. The Eyes of Divinity illuminate the Waters both by day and by night.

Immersed in deep meditation, the Spirit of the Deep absorbs its growing beauty, in endless love. In digesting all events, transforming them towards perfection, while mirroring Itself in the Eyes, Miraculous Inspiration transforms herself and She grows, both in Severity and in Mercy, and develops Her eternal knowledge.

Drinking the Light and feeding on realizations, She grows in Understanding and Wisdom and realizes that She has grown into her full potential, She has become one with Her mirror image and in an explosion of love and delight, both become one, a marriage made in Heaven.

In the country called Self-luminous Bliss, She opens her entire being for the Spirit of the Deep, like a Blue Lotus, being completely absorbed in beauty and total silence. Amidst this silence, at the end of the Timeless Hour, She builds a nest from the branches of incense trees. Laying herself down amidst the branches, Miraculous Inspiration ignites the Fire, and burns Herself through ecstasy. When that fuel is used up, only Her essence remains, an Egg, a promise of a new incarnation. Thus, She renews herself time and again, in the purifying golden fire, opening the way ...

In the country called Self-luminous Bliss the shell of the Egg breaks into four pieces and the Soul bird arises; Black in the void of the Night and Golden in the brightness of the Light, the bird travels between the Worlds unseen. It opens the way to the Caves of Consciousness, for those who want to follow her on the road of Miraculous Inspiration.

MAP OF THE ENCHANTED LANDS

Into the Deep

I like to travel and I always look and see if there are old stories about places I plan to visit. A story sometimes makes a seemingly meaningless place interesting to visit. For this reason, I once climbed Mount Cadair Idris in Wales. Among the people who had climbed this mountain before me are the magician Merlin and the poet William Butler Yeats. They wrote that if you spent the night on top of this mountain, you would change into a visionary or a poet.

So, I decided to follow in their footsteps. In my naivety, I assumed that there are worse examples to follow. I thought it might be an interesting journey, not realizing that only fools walk in areas that angels wouldn't dare to tread... So here I walk, climbing the so-called Chair of the Giant Idris. The mountain is steep; I can hear my breath getting faster. I climb the sandy path through the pine wood. I inhale the smell of mushrooms evaporating from the moist woods. Every time I touch the branches, the pine trees greet me with their spicy perfume, drifting nebula forming fragile veils that filter the sun's light. When the rays of the sun break through the mists, they create cathedrals of light. The leaves of the trees whirl on the wind, rushing, bowing and receiving the blessings of the elements. They move like dancers, engaged in a whirling duet with the ever-changing forces of nature.

With every step I climb, the landscape changes. The trees now become smaller and finally: they all disappear. In spite of the thick soles of my hiking boots, I now feel the rough rocks of the mountain path under my feet. With every turn I make, the panorama changes. The green enclosure of the woods makes way for blue distances and rough peaks. The winds change from gentle breezes into powerful gusts that chase the clouds.

Then I arrive at a crossroads in the wilderness and a strange thought enters my mind. Is my imagination playing tricks on me? There is little oxygen here, the air is thin...

I look at the road and ask: "Where are you going?"
"Where do you want to go?" answers the Way Back.
"I want to visit the miraculous. I want explore the Depth of Things."

Then the wind rises and I am standing amidst a Vortex of Wisdom. Now I very clearly hear a voice: *"Are you prepared to contact the Deep? The Deep that resides within? She is enchantingly lit with image and sound. Put your feet on this path; it is seldom set foot upon."*

A track lights up in the fog. I don't see any broken branches or footprints in the grass; only that light blue haze, that mist, which reveals the presence of angels, fairies and Gods...
I ask the voice: *"Who are you?"*

"As the steersman of the Boat of Millions of Years, I sail the Seven Seas. I am the silent witness of the rise and fall of cultures. I sail the timeless waves of the Deep. I have seen Draco fall. I was there when Osiris *lived. I saw him dying. I am the guardian of Heavenly Mountain, the Guide of the Deep."*
I sigh and try to understand what the voice tells me. I can feel the depth of the message, but I cannot get a grip on its exact meaning.

By now, I have reached the top. I sit down and look out over a spacious landscape. Night falls, the mists pull away, the skies turn blue and purple. The first stars appear and a figure manifests out of thin air. He is clothed in dark robes and thus, I can only see his outline against the dark sky. Instinctively, I step back. The hair on my neck stands up. The wind rises and I shiver when the appearance continues his speech in a low whispering voice:

"My name is Idris. Welcome to my high seat. Look around you. From here, you can oversee the Lands of Life. So far, you have only climbed my mountain from the outside, but inside of this mountain there are the great Secrets of the Deep. They are hidden in its many Caves and corridors. The Deep is timeless; it's a causal world. The changes that are made here determine what will happen in your World of Time. Every event inside my mountain takes place in the Timeless Hour and follows the laws of eternal patterns. The Heavenly Mountain is a place in the mind. I want to teach you how the Deep controls the events in your life."

"Do you know that most people are trapped in their inner worlds? Every reality, each event is created in the secret Caves of my mountain. I invite you on a journey to explore these Caves and corridors and study their enchantment. I'm going to teach you how to liberate yourself from these enchantments. Will you follow me on a journey?"

My hackles stand up. I feel the shivering of goosebumps rising on my arms, my heart is beating in anticipation.

Idris continues: *"Know that the Timeless Hour cannot be observed by everyone. Therefore, many think that the Deep does not exist. Most people are not able to transcend their everyday experiences. Only a few understand the psychological levels. Of this group, only a fraction can access the Timeless Hour and of them, only the exceptional ones can observe the movements of the Deep that determine the events in the World of Time ... and influence them!"*

Sighing, I say: *"That sounds like an interesting adventure. Yes, I want to go there and tell that story. But in order to write it down, I will need a framework."*

"The structure is that you are the student and I am the teacher..."

"That works fine for me," I answer happily.

... and Idris points at me, squeezes his eyes and says, *"... And that means you are the Fool and I am the Dog."*

§ 7. How to prepare for guided meditations

In order to enable you to make a connection with the various Caves of Consciousness, represented by the Tarot cards, I have written meditations that will help you get in tune with the different energies of the Caves. You will need to learn how to work in a light trance. If you compare the mind with an iceberg, your conscious mind is only the top that sticks out of the water. The subconscious mind is the massive unseen iceberg below the surface. The subconscious mind filters out what is going to become conscious knowledge, and it makes automatic choices for you without your conscious awareness.

Trance is not something alien. It is a natural state of consciousness that you often use during the day: when you listen to music, watch television, or drive your car on autopilot, you are in a light trance. Trance is necessary to get access to your subconscious mind and change its instructions! Changing the instructions of the subconscious mind will cause changes in your life.

The subconscious mind does not work rationally; it works with images and fantasy. When you internalize the pictures of the Tarot cards, you will be able to access the deep structures of the subconscious mind and gradually release the hidden wisdom inside. If you want to assess your current situation, or cause changes in your life, you need to 'contact' the images of the Deep Mind. Your subconscious mind first needs to learn the language of the Tarot. You will know that the subconscious mind has accepted the imagery when the cards get 'contacted'. You will know that you have successfully contacted them when they creep into your dreams and daydreams and you get meaningful new realizations. If the subconscious mind accepts the suggestions to generate awareness and a change in direction, it will start to do the work for you. In this way, you can initiate changes in your life in a way that is not an exercise in willpower.

So, you need to learn how to switch from your conscious rational awareness to a relaxed, dreamy state of light trance. You can do this by following guided meditations and rituals. The more you practice, the more effective you will become. By using the methods of the Book of the Caves, you will learn techniques that can help you improve your life.

The Tarot Journeys will take you through guided meditations and magical rituals. You will get tasks. These tasks are designed to bring you new insights and realizations, as well as unique experiences. In this way, you will build a new and unique understanding and perspective of the Tarot cards.

§ 8. Induction and relaxation

This induction and relaxation exercise is to be performed before every meditation. Make it into a good habit to take about 10 minutes for this exercise, so that you are thoroughly relaxed. The more relaxed you are, the more you will gain from your meditation. The ideal state to perform meditations in is: body asleep, mind awake. It is a matter of practice to find the right balance between being overly alert and being on the edge between waking and sleeping.

➢ Sit down in a comfortable chair and breathe deeply for a couple of times, relax, and let all the tension go. Establish a breathing rhythm of 4 counts in – 2 counts rest– 4 counts out– 2 counts rest. While you breathe in this rhythm, you will start to relax all your muscles.

➢ Leave all your worries in your daily life behind and turn your attention inwards. Go to that inner space where everything is good and beautiful, exactly as it should be.

➢ Let all the tension flow downwards into the earth.

➢ Pay close attention to the muscles in your face, your jaws, eyes, and forehead.

➢ Go downwards systematically and scan your body. Relax the muscles in your neck, scan your arms, and your fingers.

➢ Go further down and check your chest. How is the posture of your head and spine? Sit straight and balance your head on your spine.

- Go further downwards, scan your solar plexus and your belly. Do you have enough space to breathe or do tight clothing or belts keep you from breathing fully? Are you able to fill the top of your lungs with oxygen, and does your belly expand when you breathe in?
- If necessary, untie the buttons and give yourself space to breathe properly.
- Go further downwards and scan your buttocks, your upper legs, and lower legs. Look for any tense muscles and if you discover any, let the tension flow downwards through your breath into the earth.
- Finally, you have reached your feet. How do they feel? Are they warm or cold? Do they fully touch the ground? Look at your body position, your legs and feet should be parallel and your feet should be firmly on the ground.
- Let all the tension flow into the earth and feel the pulse under your feet. Realize that your pulse now synchronizes with the heartbeat of the Earth herself.
- Find that place in yourself where you always recover, where your Inner Light is burning brightly. Make a conscious contact with that Inner Light. While you concentrate on that Inner Flame, you will start to build the images that I give to you.

At the end of each meditation session, you perform a reverse exercise, to bring yourself back to being fully awake in your daily consciousness. You will find the reverse exercise at the end of the first meditation.

TRUMP O △ THE FOOL א

Trump O

The Fool on the Hill

The Spirit of the Ether

Hebrew letter **Aleph א meaning Ox**
Mother letter **Air**
Path color **Pale Yellow**

Thirty-Two Paths of Wisdom:

The Eleventh Path is the Scintillating Intelligence, because it is the essence of that curtain which is placed close to the order of the disposition, and this is a special dignity given to it that it may be able to stand before the Face of the Cause of Causes.

§ 9. Meditation: The Fool on the Hill

When you have completed your relaxation exercises, you visualize yourself sitting on a mountaintop on a moonless night. It is deep into the night, and the stars shine high above your head. You are exposed to the miraculous winds on the top of Cadair Idris. The gust tears at your clothes, and you are intrigued by a voice: you can clearly hear the voice of Idris in the rushing winds.

"Sit down and listen to the silent noise that lies in the background of Creation. Listen to the Sound beyond all sounds, and become aware of a deep silence. Listen to my voice, relax more deeply, and pay close attention, because you can hear the sound of rushing waves in the background. It is as if the noise of water is everywhere around you."

"Listen and watch attentively, and you will gradually become aware of an endlessness—a timeless, deep darkness. Feel how Eternity is around you and within you. You are completely relaxed and safe, floating joyfully in a limitless space, filled with warm, dark moisture. Do you feel how you slowly become ecstatic?"

"One with the Cause of Causes, your soul becomes completely immersed in the euphoric experience of the Deep... Do you feel a movement?" When a ripple breaks through the timeless silence, notice how a wave lifts you? It gently lifts you up from the Deep Waters.

Feel the exciting pleasure of floating, drifting, wavering... Become aware of the subtle changes caused by the movement of the waters that surround you...."

"Now you sense a change—an increasing pressure, a resistance, and a force pushing you through a warm, moist, organic substance. What do you feel? Scan your impressions. Notice that you are pressing against what appears to be a thin membrane or something like fleece..."

"Scan the space around you again and become aware that your surroundings are changing dramatically. Experience the endless above, the boundless below, the limitless before, behind, left, and right, stretching out ceaselessly into the Deep. Hear the murmuring, echoing sound of water all around you... And again... feel a push from behind, pressing you through another layer of resistance and... pass the Second Veil."

"Become aware of another phenomenon: feel how the unity is slightly shattered. You feel the strong desire to know what will happen next."
With a shock, I realize that I have a past—an experience I cannot get back to. A strange and new rhythmic sound breaks through the silence. Tick-tock, tick-tock, tick-tock... a rhythmic repetition. I wonder what this is? Idris answers immediately: *"You are passing the Veil of Time."*

The Deep moves and stirs; the sensation of pressure increases. I feel that I am being pushed through a narrow canal. I clearly hear the noise of the Third Veil breaking. A sudden brightness—I get bedazzled. Idris's voice sounds again: *"Welcome to the world of the Limitless Light."*

The shock causes me to gasp deeply, and I breathe in my first breath. I look around; the air is charged with a fine golden dust—an exquisite shower of golden energy illuminates my spirit and recharges my body. I breathe it in, fill my lungs with this Golden Breath, and feel empowered by that Scintillating Intelligence.

Everything is silent around me, but my surroundings speak to me with meaning and essence. I experience a sense of fulfillment. With every breath I take, I become increasingly aware of the realization that everything around me is sacred, loaded with sacred essence. I become aware of a fire that burns deep inside me...

§ 10. The Blessing of the Goddess

Seated at the mountaintop of Caer Idris, I survey the landscape. I become aware of yet another presence. A hand touches me while a wave of consciousness gently stirs my mind. There is no manifestation—only a conscious latency. There... I feel it again...

"Welcome to the top of my mountain. It has a secret name and function; this is the Mountain of Salvation—the famous mountain Heru. Searched for by many seekers, often sought but seldom found. It was praised by many famous writers who climbed to the top. Ah, I remember those days when Vergilius brought Dante up here, the historical visit of Wolfram von Eschenbach. My history goes back beyond Biblical times. My location is flexible because I am located in the Otherworld, and seekers can approach me from different entrances and climb me."

"You ask yourself who I am? My name is Eternity. I am the Goddess of the Deep. You are my child. I created you from Deep Water and Utter Silence. You were conceived by an act of love. After giving birth to you, I named you Heru. Your name means Light. You are the Spirit of the Tarot, the Child of the Deep Waters. Your nature is Air. When Air is warmed, it rises—just like the soul. You are the up-current of the Spirit. But before you can rise, you must descend first."

"Remember that Light causes Shadow. In Eternity, they are merged together, unified and undivided. They are pure and intense inner reflection: an endless brightness of Dark Light, filled with Joy and Bliss. In the World of the Caves, however, they are dual—like two sides of a coin, inseparable opposites. To help you remember this, I will use two colors to paint your skin: one half will be white, and the other half black. Learn how to dance with your shadow, Heru, because it is an integral part of who you are! In my magical garden of delight, you will dance the Minuet of Life in a loving embrace with

your shadow. Does your shadow have a name as well? Some will call him King Herla, or Harlequin. Others will call him Erlkönig, the King of the Elves. You are predestined to go on an adventure; I have come to give you an important task. I invite you to descend into the sacred World of the Caves."

I let these words sink in for a while. *"Why would I want to do that?"*

The answer comes immediately: *"To unfold your true potential and to gain access to the Enchanted Lands,"* Eternity answers, and she continues: *"It is almost time for your Descent, Heru, but before you go, I have some important gifts for you."*

I watch in wonder as I see a wand forming from a ray of light; a simple wooden wand materializes before my very eyes. Then Eternity speaks into my mind again:

"I give you the Batocchio; it is a wand with special qualities. It has the magical power to change the Cave you are in. It also holds hidden powers that you will discover in due time. At the end of the wand, hang this pouch. I made it myself from real chamois leather. On the pouch, I have inscribed my symbol—the All-seeing Eye in a Triangle—as a token to show that I support you and watch over you wherever you go. But in order to be successful, you must first discover the Golden Breath."

My eyes follow the gestures of Eternity with great concentration. I watch as She gathers golden specks of light from the scintillating air around me and inserts the particles into the pouch.

"These are important magical powers in your bag, Heru. They are my birth gift to you—my help on your sacred mission. These golden grains are the seeds of all your talents. They contain the sacred patterns to expand your abilities. By using them, you will be able to unfold your full potential. You must grow them in your magical garden once you have found that secret place in the center of my world. Sow them, water them, and nurture them so that they become strong and reliable skills!"

Hundreds of questions tumble around in my mind and build up an inner pressure. An urgent concern forms, and I ask: *"Why do I need to descend into the World of Matter?"* Eternity increases her pressure. Her mind-touch feels like two piercing eyes that penetrate me with an intense glance. The sphere of her communication changes and becomes meaningful. She proclaims: *"I send you downwards on a high mission, Heru. Your task is to go and search for the Patterns of the Deep, and to learn to apply their sacred laws in your life: the Laws of Divinity that Thoth wrote down in his famous magical book. Is this a contract we can agree on?"*

To my astonishment, I see a feather fall at my feet. From the clouds, thick drops of salt water create a small pool in front of me, and I watch as one of the stars from the firmament tumbles down. Again, I feel her mind-touch:
"Dip the tip of the feather into the tears I shed for you, and write your mission on your star:

Unraveling the Wisdom of the Sacred Caves."

I feel a spirit-hand touch mine. The cloudy fingers are cold and moist as they gently lay the feather in my hand. Then the misty hand points to the star: *"Sign here."*

Do I do what she asks of me? She smiles, picks up the star again, and places it into the pouch.

"My gifts are precious," Eternity continues. *"You will learn how to use these keys when the time is right. But first, place the feather I gave you on your hat. It is the Feather of Truth. This is your compass needle–it will always point to your True North. Furthermore, you will need these."*

On the top of the mountain, a ray of light singles out four stones and a conch shell. The stones are smoothly polished, except for the strange triangles engraved on their surfaces.

"These stones are keys to unlock the Secrets of the Universe. I am also giving you this conch shell. It is a roadmap to finding your Way Back. Last but not least, I will give you a friend. Idris will open the ways for you and show you the road when the path is unclear. Ah, you are wondering who Idris is? Idris is a shapeshifter. On the Inner Planes, he is a powerful wizard and a wise mage. In the world of materialization, he can appear

as a man, a jackal, or a dog. He can speak in the winds or in the rushing sounds of water. He can manifest as a king or a beggar. Idris has a special talent, he can always find Water in the Wilderness."

"There is one more task I lay upon your shoulders, Heru." Eternity's misty hand now shows me a golden ring. *"This golden ring is a magical relic with enormous powers. This is not a gift, Heru; it is a reward. You must earn this magical golden ring by fulfilling twelve tasks and passing twelve tests."*

I become sharply aware of the inclement weather. The cutting winds feel like sharp, cold razors on my skin; they pull at my clothes. The mists have gathered in the valley below, and seen from this high, exposed mountaintop, they resemble an ocean in the sky.

Then Eternity speaks again: *"Heru, I am sending you on a mission. You need to retrieve the Golden Ring from the Enchanted Lands. You will see glimpses of its existence as your adventures unfold. When you pass the Twelve Tests, the Ring will be yours."*

I watch in amazement as the misty spirit-hand throws the Ring into the fathomless depths. I hear its ringing sound disappear into the void.

"Enough for now. I feel many questions tumbling around in your mind. There are many riddles waiting to be solved. Are you willing to go on this adventure? Make your

decision... now! Prepare for your Descent, Heru. An important task lies ahead. You must work like an ox, plough the earth, and turn the wilderness of your life into a fertile place where your soul can unfold its full potential. Turn your life into a space where everything that is sown grows abundantly. And don't forget to work with the gifts I gave you, for that is your birthright!"

Then the mind-touch is gone, and I am alone on the mountaintop. I take the pouch from the Batocchio, open it, and check what is inside. In the palm of my hand, I hold a handful of glittering seeds, four cobblestones, a conch shell, and a swan feather. The silence is broken by a barking sound in the distance, and an enthusiastic black dog comes rushing toward me and jumps up against my legs. I cuddle him. Where does he come from? There is no one nearby on this lonely mountaintop.

"Ouch!" I feel a sudden sharp pain in my left foot. My arm automatically lashes out at the dog, for it has bitten me on the ankle, wounding my heel... I even limp slightly. But the animal is enthusiastic and wants to play. When I bend over to pat him, I see that he wears a collar. I look to see if anything is written on it. Who is the owner of this dog? I feel the outline of letters engraved in the leather. When I crouch down to read it, the dog enthusiastically tries to lick my face. My heart starts to race when I read what is written on it: Idris!

"So, you will show me the way?" I say to the dog. *"I wonder where you will take me..."* I rise, place the hat on my head, attach the pouch to the end of the Batocchio, and lay it on my shoulder.
"Idris, I am ready to go!"
"Then knock with your Batocchio on the floor beneath you, and you will change your reality, for this is the magical power of your wand! "It is time to return to the outer world, Heru. Tap with your wand, and you will return to the profane—into the Here-and-Now."

I tap three times on the floor with my wand. I feel how the waters enclose me again, and I tumble downwards into the waterfall. All around me, splashing water rushes. I become aware of my physical surroundings. I feel my body. I stretch my muscles as I wake up in the physical world—feeling great.

§ 11. How to work with this meditation

The seed sentence to work with after this pathworking is:

My essence is Light
My radiance causes shadow
While walking my journey through Life
I dance with my Shadow

*****

The Descent
If you want more in-depth meditations on the Journey of the Fool, take a look at the website, there is an entire video training on this tarot card: https://www.hermeticartsandsciences.org/product/video/

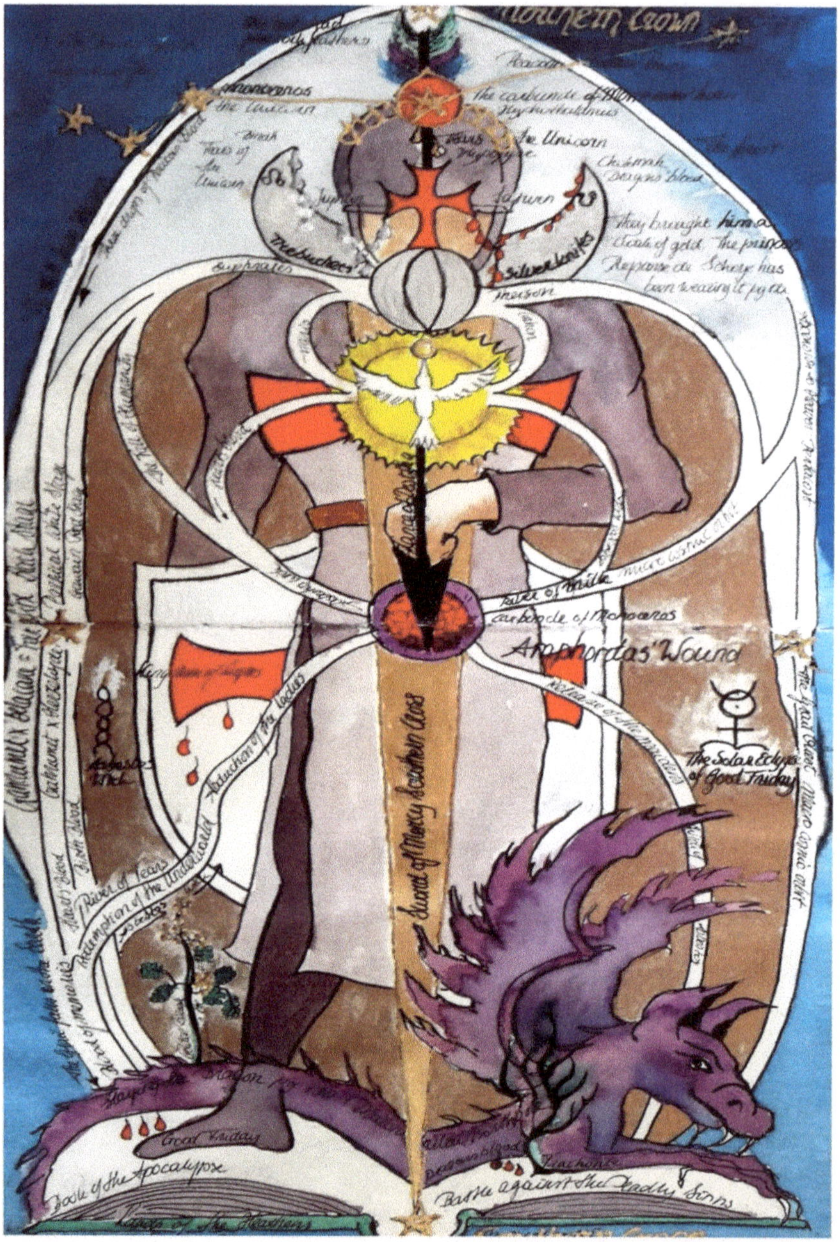

TRUMP IV ♈ THE FISHERKING ה

Trump IV – Aries – ♈

The Fisher King

The Chief among the Mighty

Hebrew letter **Heh ה meaning Window**
Simple Letter: **Sight**
Path color **Scarlet**
Sign **Aries ♈**

Thirty-Two Paths of Wisdom:

The Fifteenth Path is the Constituting Intelligence, so called because it constitutes the substance of creation in pure darkness, and men have spoken of these contemplations: it is that darkness spoken of in Scripture, Job xxxviii.9. "and thick darkness a swaddling band for it".

...The mists enclose me, I try to follow Idris. I hear him in the distance—his barking is muffled by the thick fog. Then, suddenly, I slip on a slippery stone, and I tumble into a stream of swirling water, taking me downwards. It is scary because the mists prevent me from seeing my surroundings. Everywhere around me, I feel splashing water and rocks. I feel myself rushing through a dark Abyss of vast space. I enter into the dream between the worlds. I see my past as a quick video of previous dramas, played at double speed. I am falling through a kaleidoscope of endless possibilities; around me, images appear of all times. I get glimpses of unlimited choices, impressions of immeasurable futures. Falling into that bottomless emptiness, I hear a voice echoing:

"Who are you, Heru? And what do you want? What is your mission, Heru? Is there anything you can imagine that is worth living for?"

In my dream, I am carried away by one of the rivers that rush powerfully downwards from the heights of the Mountain of Salvation. I am completely and wonderfully surrounded by water, and I experience how my spirit is being carried.

"Carried? By whom?"
As soon as I think that, I hear the answer in the rushing noise. I hear the voice of the Wind of the Spirit that carries me downwards. The Infalling Light of Realization tells me:

"I am the River of Truth. My possibilities are endless. I carry you to your destiny. Speak a word or imagine a world, and I will carry you into another reality. One single word can switch my course. I carry you towards your hopes and dreams. What do you want, Heru? A life to run from fear, or do you want to embrace your life? I will carry you to that reality where you can learn."

And suddenly, I land in a big, empty hall. The hall is shaped like a perfect cube. The walls are built from beautiful black star obsidian. Around me, the bright lights of stars are shining—they radiate with wisdom. To my left and right, the roof is upheld by huge pillars. This is where I will build my Inner Space. The hall has no furniture, but it has strange decorations. I look around me to take in my surroundings. The floor is paved with black and white tiles. The ceiling is painted lapis lazuli blue, and in the exact center, a large rose is painted. In each of the walls of the room, there is a series of three stained-glass doors, with the sign of the Zodiac depicted above each entrance.

I take my seat here in this magical hall. In the center of the hall, there stands an empty chair, also in the shape of a cube. Next to the chair, Idris is waiting. I feel his mind-touch, and strange ideas begin to spread in my mind:

"You have found the Hall of the Mountain King, Heru - that is great! This is the place where your first task will start. Take your seat on this cube. It is located exactly in the Centre of your Universe. You have entered Eternal Time, at the time of the Dawn of

Humanity. This is the time when the Gods walk the Earth—when everything is exactly as it is supposed to be. This is a place of great magic... that means, as long as you are able to control and wield the enormous forces that surround you. Your first task is to structure these enormous forces."

I look around me. I feel that I am surrounded by chaos, and I feel helpless in a hostile environment with unknown rules, amidst the violent forces of a creation coming into existence. This is a dangerous environment for a simple soul like me, newly born from the Light. But I take the task upon myself. I will learn to rule responsibly, and weigh different interests, fates, and possibilities—for that is the best hope for fulfilment and peace that I can imagine.

§ 12. The Wounded King

I receive a vision: under my leadership, I will give form to the dream I want to manifest—a dream of a Universe without war, where angels from all the different heavens, gods from all cultures, and souls descending from all the different bloodlines can live together in mutual respect. I take my seat on the cubical throne, and I feel the overshadowing of a strange entity...

"I am the oldest of Kings, the Ancient of Days, belonging to those beings who are older than time. I date from the time before Time was created. I take up my Wand of Power—

it is topped with a ram's head—and I am putting all the patterns, which are created by my consort, the Empress, into their rightful place."

A sharp, shrieking voice fills the entire hall. The walls resonate, and my heart shrinks as I listen to the message: *"A time without war? A time without me, the Opposer? No way!"*

And to my shock and bewilderment, King Herla manifests in front of me. He is clothed in a medieval outfit. In one hand he holds a lance; in the other, a flask with a green fluid in it. He looks straight into my eyes with a haggard glance—his eyes shoot fire: *"Never forget that I have a sacred mission as well, Heru. My task is to cause friction. Without friction, development isn't even possible! I am your other half—never underestimate me. I am the shadow on your face, your dark Self, causing havoc and chaos in your unconscious mind. You will never get rid of me, because I am your survival when the circumstances become dangerous. In order for you to remember me, I have brought my lance, the Lance of Destiny. With this lance, I am going to wound you."*

And Herla takes the Lance of Destiny in both his hands. He hits the ground running and charges at me. He strikes me right in my groin. Then he uncorks the bottle and pours the green fluid into my wound. Herla turns around and disappears into thin air.

I cringe in pain. The wound is bleeding profusely. To my dismay, the wound is deep and full of dirt. This is a nasty injury; it might get infected. I feel the blood streaming from my body, and instead of taking my seat on a throne, I ask the Inner Planes to bring me a bed to lie on.

§ 13. Meditation: The Wounded King

While I am resting here and trying to staunch the bleeding, I hear the voice of Idris: *"You are a King, Heru, but for now you are a wounded king. Before you start to rule the Enchanted Lands, you first need to heal yourself from your psychic wounds. Only when you are able to heal the King can you heal your Enchanted Lands... I have an assignment for you. Meditate on your life, and visualize yourself falling from heaven. At the bottom end of the Fall, you hit the Nadir of your life. What is the existential wound in need of healing that determines your life?"*

Then I think of the magical powers of my Batocchio. I want to change my reality. I tap three times with my wand on the floor. I feel how the waters enclose me, and I tumble downwards into the waterfall again. Everywhere around me, I see splashing water rushing through the Abyss of vast space. Again, I enter the dream between the worlds and fall through endless possibilities. I feel all kinds of desires. I see images of myself in all times—past and future. I get glimpses of endless choices. Falling into that bottomless emptiness, I hear the voice echoing again: *"Who are you, Heru? A wounded King? A Fool on a Hill? And what do you desire? Is there anything you can imagine that is worth living for?"*

And with that question, I am left alone. I feel a strong desire as the images fade away... In the distance, I hear the words of Idris: *"It is time to return to the outer world, Heru. Tap with your wand and you will return to your own world, into the Here-and-Now."*

I tap three times on the floor with my wand. I feel how the waters enclose me again, and I tumble downwards into the waterfall once more. Everywhere around me, I see splashing water rushing around me. I become aware of my physical surroundings. I feel my body, I stretch my muscles, and I wake up in the physical world, feeling great.

V ♉ THE HIGH PRIEST ו

Trump V – Taurus - ♉

The High Priest

The Magus of the Eternal

Hebrew letter	**Vav ו meaning Nail**
Simple letter	**Hearing**
Path color	**Red-orange**
Sign	**Taurus ♉**

Thirty-Two Paths of Wisdom:

The Sixteenth Path is the Triumphal or Eternal Intelligence, so called because it is the pleasure of the Glory, beyond which is no other Glory like to it, and it is called also the Paradise prepared for the Righteous.

… I prepare myself for the next journey into the Reality beyond Time. I sit down in my meditation room and I tap with my Batocchio on the floor. I feel how the mists enclose me again, like the previous time. If this wand is able to change my reality, where will it bring me now? I hear Idris barking in the distance; I try to follow him. Once again, I am swept away by the waters and embedded in thick fog. I try to get some orientation about where I am going, but it is impossible; the nebula doesn't allow me to see any further than 10 meters. The atmosphere is tense, loaded with desire and expectation. A tingling sensation rushes through my body. Again, I travel through the many dreams between the worlds. I see crises unfold; I witness how loves blossom and decay. I see coming changes on the World's stage. I remember past lives. Once again, I fall through myriads of possibilities, slide between aeons of time, and I get glimpses of unlimited choices. Then I hear the voice again: *"Who are you, Heru? And what do you want? What is your mission, Heru? Is there anything you can imagine that is worth living for?"*

Then I arrive at a double door. It is an old door made of wood. It has big iron hinges and a large iron knocker. Since I can't think of anything else to do, I decide to knock on the door. I hear footsteps approaching on tiles and then the sound of creaking iron and old wood. One side of the double door opens slowly, and an old bearded figure appears from behind the door. He is clothed in long robes and wears a hooded mantle. His back is bent because of his old age. He looks straight into my eyes and says: *"Yes? What can I do for you?"*

I answer: *"My name is Heru, I come from the profane world. I have climbed the Mountain of Salvation. I have travelled through thick mists and I was carried by rushing water. I tapped the ground with my Bastocchio and arrived at this door."*
"Oh well, are you one of those? Then answer this question for me: Is there anything you can imagine that is worth living for?"

I feel the courage sinking into my shoes. My back bends and I sigh: *"This is what I try to figure out. I am looking for my life's mission. That is why I travel through the Worlds of Dreams."*
The greybeard bends his head and lifts his hand in a questioning gesture: *"Where were you before you arrived here?"*

"First, I climbed the Mountain of Salvation where Eternity sent me on a mission to find the Golden Ring that she threw into the Waters of Space. Then I was swept away by a running river and arrived in a great hall between the Worlds. It was called the Hall of the Mountain King. There I witnessed a great king becoming severely wounded by a criminal who called himself King Herla. I merged with this Wounded King and was given a task: to heal the Wound of the King and in this way heal the Enchanted Land."

"Ah, you come from the Hall of the Mountain King. Let me introduce myself to you. My name is Idris."

I am confused: does this chap have the same name as my dog? What is this place? Where am I?

"I can read your thoughts, Heru. I am the black dog: I am Idris the Mage. I am a shapeshifter. You will encounter me during your journey in many disguises. Now that you have arrived here at this Door between the Worlds, I will disclose the nature of this sacred place to you. On top of the Mountain of Salvation, there is the entrance to a magical castle: it is the famous Grail Castle. Few people manage to find the entrance to this mysterious building. Even fewer people are allowed entrance. Do you know the Spell that gives you access to this magical realm?"

I shake my head; I have never heard of anything like this. I lift my head in anticipation.
"When you use your Bastocchio to enter a different reality, you can give it directions where it must take you. One of the destinations is the Hall of the Mountain King. It is the central hall of the Grail Castle, the place where you shared your fate with the Wounded King. When you say this spell and tap on the floor with your Bastocchio, you enter into the Hall of the Mountain King."
Idris takes my hand and instructs me to tap my wand while I repeat after him:

Now do I descend into the Inner Seas
Whose Waters rise and fall within my soul
Now let the Inner Elements be seduced and still

Let me immerse myself into those Living Waters
And emerging therefrom
Let me bring from latent stress to potent image
The symbol of the King's High Table.[1]

The double doors swing open, the nebula drifts apart, and I step into the Great Hall with the black and white tiled floor and the stained-glass doors. Nothing has changed; the Wounded King is still writhing on his bed, severely ill. He has issued a decree that calls for the best doctors in the world to heal the severe wound in his groin. But suddenly I notice that one thing has changed. One of the stained-glass doors is lit. I can clearly see that the morning sun of an early spring shines from behind the door and illuminates the stained glass. I clearly see the representation on the stained glass; it shows an image of the Fisher King. Above the door is a representation of the constellation Aries - ♈ -.

"Yes", says Idris: *"The first one of the Great Lights burns bright, the test of the Constellation Aries determines the rest of your journey, to seek healing for the Wounded King. His fate is your fate. When you manage to heal the wound that you sustained when you fell from Heaven, you are on the right track. So once again I ask you: Who are you,*

---

[1] W.E. Butler, SOL course

Heru? And what do you want? What is your mission, Heru? Is there anything you can imagine that is worth living for?"
I sigh and, on impulse, I answer: *"To heal the Wounded King, to restore the fertility in the Enchanted Lands, and to ignite my Inner Light."*

Then I see the Sun outside the hall moving; it moves towards the next stained-glass door, so that it now illuminates the image there. It is the image of the High Priest. Above the door there is the representation of the Constellation Taurus - ♉ -. On the Eastern wall, between the stained-glass doors of Aries and Taurus, a wide golden band appears, connecting the two doors. Then the Door of Taurus swings open. Idris gestures to follow him through. On the other side of the door there is a bridge. Next to the bridge there is a sign indicating the name of the bridge. I walk towards it to read it. On it there is written:

Triumphant Intelligence
Bridge between Wisdom and Rulership

Strange words that appear to have no meaning. But the bridge looks very interesting. I decide to cross it, and I see that it crosses an enormously deep abyss. Above me a rainbow appears in the skies, and I feel and hear the whispering sounds of the Winds of Wisdom all around me. Then I become aware that I am actually walking on the Rainbow, ever upwards in a myriad of colors. I feel the winds rise around me, four winds coming from the four cardinal directions, together making a whispering sound, as if in this silence words are spoken. The whispering sounds of the winds start to make sense. I can hear a voice. At first, it is very quiet and distant, but gradually I understand the message that is given to me more clearly.

§ 14. The Bridge between the Worlds

While I am walking this Rainbow Bridge, I become aware of the beauty of the landscape that surrounds me. The Whitsun light of the Spiritual Sun illuminates the scene and rainbow-colored clouds in strange shapes drift above me and around me. Suddenly the clouds gather together and I find myself surrounded by the nebula. I become aware of a curious feeling. I investigate it and when I open my mind to it, a flow of knowledge and wisdom is transmitted unto me. I become more and more encapsulated by the rainbow colors and I wonder where this road will bring me.

Suddenly I see another building looming up. The doors of the building swing open, and I arrive in a large hall. My footsteps echo and the entire atmosphere is scintillating with a sphere of expectation...

§ 15. The Throne Hall

In the middle of the hall, I see a tall and imposing figure sitting on a throne. The aura of this person fills the entire hall. I feel the energy going through me, bubbling like champagne. Suddenly the tall figure looks into my eyes, and I become so awestruck that I bow instinctively. I fall on my knees and carefully look up, to get another glimpse of the pure power that comes towards me through the radiating eyes of the imposing priest. He is sitting on a High Throne amidst two pillars.

I hear his words; they are transmitted mentally. No word is spoken aloud, no sound breaks the deep silence, but in my mind a world of joy opens and my heart starts to dance on the flow of wisdom, while sacred words are telepathically communicated to me.

§ 16. The High Priest

"Welcome Heru, I have been expecting you," says the priest on the throne.
I raise my eyebrows: *"Who are you?"*
"I am the Hierophant," is the answer: *"I have called you to me because I want to teach you the sacredness of all things. The fact that you have found me tells me that you are a soul on a divine mission. You live your life in the Profane World of Matter, but your task is to manifest your highest mission. I have knowledge that you need. I am the bridge*

builder, the Pontifex. I will teach you how to connect your experiences in the world of matter to your quest for Inner Illumination."

I turn my head sideways and scratch my head. With a sigh, I look into the eyes of the priest: *"What are you exactly?"* I ask the Hierophant. *"I have never met a Hierophant before. What is your function?"*

"Dear Heru," the Hierophant answers: *"I am the head of the Temple of the Mysteries, similar to the Pope who is the head of a religion in the world. I am connected to the Sacred Bull Meskethiu, the Great Bull of the Skies who guarded the deepest mysteries that are hidden in the North Pole Heavens in the far past."*

I shake my head and breathe in: *"Why does the world need a Hierophant when we already have a Pope?"*

"The Pope and his colleagues are leaders of a herd. They lead the tribe over the safe roads of natural spiritual development into the future. I - the Hierophant - train initiates. Are you such a seeker, Heru? Because if you are, I will train you to take responsibility for yourself, rather than depend on the choices made by those around you, and share their fate. Religious seekers follow priests through faith. Are you a religious seeker or a potential initiate? Do you search for the road of initiation? If you are, I will train you. I will teach you how to find your own way. I will teach you how to generate illuminating

experiences and how to connect them to the Sacred Teachings of all Ages. In this way, you will experience Inner Riches. Religions teach exoteric knowledge to lay people. In contrast to this, I train seekers to open themselves to esoteric teachings by showing them the way to Inner Illumination."

I look into his eyes; this High Priest feels to me like a father figure. He communicates Wisdom to me. I recognize him as my Inner Teacher who makes me understand the Sacredness around me and inside of me so that I can act accordingly.

§ 17. The Inner Voice

While I am sitting before this imposing figure, I notice that my inner ear starts to hear more: I become aware of more Inner Voices. The Hierophant tells me to listen and learn how to recognize them. I hear the voices of beings that are so much wiser than myself. With the help and the directions of the High Priest, I learn how to tune into the different waves of consciousness in my mind. I learn to listen to these different 'channels of wisdom', like a radio that can receive different radio stations. I become aware of the healing and loving vibes from higher and wiser beings than myself who transmit their wisdom and knowledge to me. While no audible sound disturbs the silence, I watch the Hierophant sitting in silence on his throne, and listen to the eternal wisdom that he communicates to me telepathically.

§ 18. The Two Sacred Keys

"You must know, Heru, that there are two important keys to the Sacred Wisdom. One key is made of pure silver. This key is connected to the Wisdom of the Moon. It is the key to your subconscious mind. You can access this realm in your dreams, in your imagination and through guided meditations. The second key is made of pure gold. This key is connected to the Wisdom of the Sun, which is located in your heart. Use the Wisdom of your heart, your Inner Sun, and through your creative imagination, get access to the Wisdom of the Moon, and you will become aware of a higher rate of vibration. Learn to use the powers of your subconscious mind to investigate the Superconscious realms Above the Sun – the wisdom that is stored in the Constellations and the Fixed Stars. Lift your consciousness beyond the limitations of time. Learn to apply eternal principles instead! Your knowledge will transcend to super-consciousness. This possibility is dormant in every human being; you only need to re-member who you are. When you do that, you will in time become a Hierophant yourself. Now I will teach you how I - as the High Priest - am connected to the constellation of Taurus in the Starry Heavens."

Spellbound, I sit at the feet of this spiritual teacher. He truly is the Magus of the Eternal. I listen to his infallible words. I cannot do anything else but listen while he shares his wisdom with me. I feel the might of the Throne he embodies, while he teaches me the structuring principles of the Sacred Knowledge.

§ 19. The Constellation Taurus

"The Horns of Taurus are connected to the Horns of the Moon. In this way, I create the Cornucopia: the Horn of Abundance. When the Sun visits my star sign and illuminates my heart, it is crowned by the Horns of Taurus. That is the time of year when the Universe pours out new life on Earth in all its forms. When the Sun visits my star sign Taurus, it radiates the maximum amount of Prana, Life Force. At that same time, the Moon in this sign enables you to receive the maximum of Universal Consciousness. Realize that in the season of Taurus, the imaginative and the generating powers are both at their maximum. Then you will hear my voice more clearly and I will teach you about the Eternal Powers."

§ 20. The Crown

I sit at the feet of this powerful teacher and my imagination is flooded with images. My heart fills itself with hope and joy. My mind is boggled with questions. I ask the Hierophant: *"You told me about your keys, but what about your Crown and your Wand of Office?"*

"My Crown is aligned to all the Powers of the Universe. It creates a connection between the 'Star Chamber of Isis' in my brain and the North Pole Constellations, the Gods, and the Zodiac belt. Thus, I am able to receive and connect all the wisdom that is emitted by the Creator of the All. My Crown is made of three layers. The first layer connects me to

the constellations of the Zodiac, the second layer transmits the Wisdom of the Elohim to me, and the top of the Crown aligns me to the Three-in-One. Every one of these forces has the form of one of the Hebrew Letters. In this way, I receive the Word of God."

§ 21. The Nail

"Heru, I have something else of importance to tell you: one of my secret names is 'Nail'. I am a bridge-builder, I connect things. I teach you how to nail the Word of the Cause of Causes to the altar of your heart. I connect you to your memory of Cosmic Unity, the World of Bliss, from whence you came, before you descended as the Fool. I teach you how to nail the Below to the Above, so that your experiences lead to your Inner Illumination, because I am the archetypical Teacher."

"The tool that I use to teach you, is my Wand of Office; it is called the Golden Bough. This fire staff raises the energies of consciousness. It illuminates the Underworld. In a later stage, I will teach you how to use the Golden Bough. For now, remember that this is the wand that Vergilius had to harvest with the help of the Sybille, in order to visit the Underworld and unite with his ancestors. But there is one greater mystery I want to hint at: the Nail. It is the tool to execute the Sacrifice."

I ask the High Priest what his name is, and he answers: *"This is the wrong question, Heru. High Priest is a function. There are different types of High Priests whose job it is to teach a certain form of Enlightenment. I am the High Priest of Ra, and I am the wr ḫrp ḥm.w n Rʿ,*  *,*[2] *which means 'The Greatest of the Seers'. I am the Mouthpiece of the Opener of the Ways. With his hands he protects my golden heart against all negativity and evil. He is my great inspiration. Through him I hear the instructions of the Eternal Mind and translate them for the Initiates, Priests, Seers and Oracles who interact with the mundane world."*

"The Sun and the Moon are the important keys, but the Key of Keys is the Heart. My Golden Heart is winged. It is depicted as an Eye in a Triangle. All these symbols point to the higher qualities of the Heart. The Light of Beauty shines through it and sees the world. It is that Light that shines through the Heart which is called is the Light of the Opener of the Ways. When He comes through, he radiates his essence into the world as the Beloved and spreads his loving essence."

Then the High Priest disappears when the nebula between the worlds encloses him. I sigh, turn around and look into the eyes of Idris.

---

[2] **wr ḫrp ḥm.w n Rʿ**
This phrase can be broken down as:

- **wr** – "great" or "greatest"
- **ḫrp** – "controller" or "overseer"
- **ḥm.w** – "servants" (literally "bodies")
- **n Rʿ** – "of Ra"

The title is pronounced as "wer kheper hemu en Ra"

"Time to return to the Great Hall", he says, while he turns around. *"Heru, can you take the branch that the Hierophant left behind?"*
I look at the floor and there is a branch of oakwood lying on the floor. It is encircled with mistletoe. In the mistletoe there are golden berries. I take the branch and give it to Idris, who uses it as a walking stick.
"Why do we take this with us, Idris?" I ask. It looks like an ordinary branch that we can pick up anywhere in the woods.
Idris nods his head, he points at the branch and with a high voice he says: *"This is the famous Golden Bough, Heru. It has many uses, which you will study later. One of its magical powers is that it can illuminate the darkness."*

Then we walk back from where we came, downwards over the rainbow bridge. Soon we are back in the forecourt of Hall of the Mountain King. While waiting in front of the stained-glass door, Idris instructs me: "*Heru, I have an assignment for you, something that you need to practice when you are back in the mundane world. It is a little spell that you can repeat at odd moments during the day, to make you aware of the Enchanted World, so that you can enter the Enchanted Lands at any time you choose. This magical reality lies just a shift of consciousness away, beyond the Veil Between the Worlds.*

§ 22. Meditation: The Inner Light

I ignite my Inner Light
I open myself to Its riches and beauty
Because with them I weave hopes and dreams
For they are the warp and weft; the real forces of creation.

Then the stained-glass door swings open, the nebula drift apart and I step into the Great Hall with the black and white tiled floor and the stained-glass doors. The Wounded King is on his bed, writhing and moaning. He is still severely ill and calls out for everyone in the world to search for ways to heal the deep bleeding wound in his groins. I greet him and assure him that I am doing my utmost to find a solution. I tell him what I have discovered so far: *"My dear King, I have contacted my Inner Teacher and he taught me that it is important to become responsible for my Inner Light. He told me that it does not help to shift the responsibility for psychic or physical pain to King Herla who caused this. He taught me to take responsibility for healing myself. He gave me a magical instrument, the Golden Bough, which can illuminate the darkness. It uses hope and dreams as the warp and the weft of the creating forces that structure the Universe. Let me give you the Golden Bough, maybe it can help to heal your severe wound."*

The king groans and carefully turns around a little bit, so that he can look at me. His fragile hands rearrange the fur cover on his body. He lifts his beard above the fur blanket, while he breathes heavily. Then he says: *"Thank you, Heru, this gift will certainly help to lift my spirits, but these healing tools are not strong enough yet to heal me. As long as we do not know how to use it exactly, the Golden Bough will ease the pain, but not heal my wound."*

Then Idris speaks: *"For now it is time to return to the outer world, Heru. Tap with your wand while you repeat the spell and you will return to your own world, into the Here-and-Now."*

I tap three times with my wand on the floor. I feel how the waters enclose me, and I tumble downwards into the waterfall again. Everywhere I see splashing water rushing around me. I become aware of my physical surroundings. I feel my body, I stretch my muscles while I repeat the spell, I wake up in the physical world, feeling great.

VI ♊ THE LOVERS ז

Trump VI – Gemini - ♊

The Lovers

The Oracle of the Mighty Gods

Hebrew letter	**Zain ז meaning Sword or Armor**
Simple Letter	**Smell**
Path color	**Orange**
Sign	**Gemini ♊**

Thirty-Two Paths of Wisdom:

The Seventeenth Path is the Disposing Intelligence, which provides Faith to the Righteous, and they are clothed with the Holy Spirit by it, and it is called the Foundation of Excellence in the State of Higher Things.

I feel that it is time to take the next journey to the Hall of the Mountain King. I take my Batocchio in my hand and I repeat the spell that Idris taught me: I visualize the Double Doors in front of me. I tap three times with the wand on the floor and whisper:

Now do I descend into the Inner Seas
Whose Waters rise and fall within my soul
Now let the Inner Elements be seduced and still
Let me immerse myself into those Living Waters
And emerging therefrom
Let me bring from latent stress to potent image
The symbol of the King's High Table.

Then Idris enters into the Great Hall, powerful and passionate and with a quick pace he arrives in the Great Hall. *"Ah, you are already here. I was held up on the Inner Planes for a short time. But now that I am here, I will need to rearrange the Great Hall a bit, to start the Work on the next level."*

Idris taps with his wand on the floor and I watch how a nebula appears and solidifies in the center of the Great Hall. It takes the form of a great Round Table that manifests in the center of the Great Hall. Idris taps on my shoulder and gestures to follow him and take a closer look at the table. "*It is a priceless object. This Round Table is made of pure blue lapis lazuli gemstone. The surface is speckled with small golden glittering sparks. Take a closer look, there are inscriptions in the surface of the Table.*"

I step forward and see that there are twelve golden lines inscribed. In each of the sections I recognize the symbols for the Zodiac: Aries ♈ , Taurus ♉, Gemini ♊, Cancer ♋, Leo ♌, Virgo ♍, Libra ♎, Scorpio ♏, Sagittarius ♐, Capricorn ♑, Aquarius ♒ and Pisces ♓.

Then Idris points at the stained-glass doors in the walls. "*Directly opposite of the section of Aries on the Round Table there is the stained-glass door of Aries in the wall. Opposite of Taurus is the door of Taurus and so on, arranged clockwise around the hall. In the Eastern wall there are Aries ♈, Taurus ♉ and Gemini ♊. In the Southern wall you will find Cancer ♋, Leo ♌ and Virgo ♍. In the Western Wall there are Libra ♎, Scorpio ♏ and Sagittarius ♐. And finally in the Northern Wall you can find Capricorn ♑, Aquarius ♒ and Pisces ♓. The doors and the Table are exactly outlined on the seasons of the year. So, the segment of Aries, Taurus and Gemini is exactly aligned to Morning and the Spring Season. The Southern wall to Noon and Summer. The West to Evening and Autumn and finally the Northern wall is aligned with Night and Winter. This great hall is the Hall of the Mountain King, but it is also called the Great Hall of the Sun. As the Sun moves through the seasons, it illuminates the glass doors one by one. The last time you visited the hall it was the season of Taurus. But now time has moved on, and it is now possible to open the Doors to Gemini.*"

I watch the Sun moving outside the hall and see how the stained-glass doors of Gemini become illuminated. Another interesting detail is that when that happens, a broad golden band forms on the wall connecting the doors of Taurus and Gemini. I can now clearly see the representation on the stained glass; it depicts an image of two Lovers. Above the doors there is a representation of the constellation Gemini II. When the Sun fully illuminates the doors of Gemini, they swing open and create a portal to an unknown reality.

"We are now able to visit the next Cave, Heru. After our adventures in Aries and Taurus, we are invited to visit the Cave of the Lovers. Everyone needs love, but love can cause both ecstasy and deep pain. Before you enter this Cave of Consciousness, you need to contemplate seriously what you desire. What version of Love are you going to manifest, and will this love be able to heal the King?"

I follow Idris and step through the portal. Again, I enter the dream between the worlds and fall through endless possibilities. I feel all kinds of desires. I search my soul to determine what type of love I seek. Who will become my Beloved One? I search through my memory, and conclude that in my past I didn't always choose wisely. Great looks, wealth are not always signs of a great character or an opportunity to grow. What situations did I find myself in? I remember what Idris told me when he instructed me before I set out on this adventure, a Cave of Consciousness is like the setting of a play. It is like a stage. The scenery is ready for the performance. The play starts when the players step on the stage. But in which play will I play the lead role? I don't want to end up in years of betrayal and abuse, addiction to pain, psychic imbalance. I have to choose wisely... I am pulled into a whirlpool and I get glimpses of endless choices. Falling into that bottomless emptiness I hear the voice again, echoing: *"Who are you, Heru? A Wounded King? A Fool on a Hill, a wise teacher? And what do you desire? Is there anything you can imagine that is worth living for?"*

And with that question, I feel a strong desire, while the images fade away... From clouds of astral matter, a new figure appears. I watch the light changing and an entity forms above the clouds. He hands me a pomegranate. *"Eat the seeds of this fruit, Heru, before you arrive in the next Cave".*

The landscape now looks entirely surrealistic. The clouds color from yellow to orange, blood red and purple. I notice that the Sun is setting and the shadows lengthen. Two enormous shadows fall over the landscape and in between them appears a path into the Otherworld.

I hesitate to follow the way, because what I see in front of me is not a normal road, but a Sword of Cosmic size stretches before my Inner Eye... I'm facing the Sword Bridge. I can only reach the other side by walking over the sharp edge of the Sword. There is no fence to protect me from falling into the deep Abyss.

"Don't be afraid, Heru", the trusted voice of Idris whispers into my inner ear. *"You have found the right entrance to the Otherworld, the road between the arms of the Star goddess. This pathway will lead you away from the Exalted Sphere of Pure Cosmic*

Consciousness and bring you into the Temple of the Heart which is built in the middle of the Sacred Garden of your Soul."

§ 23. The Sword

I start to walk the Sword bridge, and with my first step I feel the electric energy, I am amidst flashing lights. The lights zigzag and the entire atmosphere smells like I am in the middle of a thunderstorm. With every step I realize that I'm leaving the world of Divinity and I feel lonely, lost, and torn apart. Below me I see the fires taking shapes. Stars are born before my eyes. I watch the beauty of Cosmic Explosions when the Universe comes into being. The fiery energy of the Sword bridge cleaves, cuts and divides.

I pass two guardians: a red lion and an eagle watching this road. I am able to pass them without trouble, but I notice that after this point the fires change into astral shapes. While I walk this surrealistic road I wonder where I am going. Promptly the Voice answers: *"You are invited to a marriage ceremony"*.

§ 24. Hieros Gamos

Then I witness an event of intense beauty. Before my eyes the Golden Sun approaches the New Moon. I witness the first fragile kiss when they start their cosmic embrace. The colors deepen; the landscape becomes totally silent. The electricity becomes a whirlpool of emotion and ecstasy. The colors flash when they unite and a corona of golden fire lights up the scene; I am standing in a blast of pure cosmic love! The Cosmic King and Queen are united in love.

Then I hear the Voice of Idris again. *"In reality, there is only one Lover. Its name is 'Light in Darkness', or 'Night in Day'. Those are your mental states, Heru. The Marriage of the Sun and the Moon is the unification of Duality, the Sword that Divides them is a paradox."*

"Look at the love affair between the Sun and the Moon, and meditate on the duality within you. The Sun is your male side: your conscious mind which you need in the world. The Moon is your female side, your subconscious mind. Your male side admires the beauty of the Inner Woman; he falls for the Goddess of Love. He meets her in the depths of his meditation, in the wondrous world of dreams, while the Inner Woman looks upwards into the Cosmos, and looks into my eyes."

"And who are you, Idris?" I ask the Voice.
"*I have many names*", Idris answers, "*but you might know me under my name of Eros. When the Sun and Moon marry, you achieve the total integration of the Self, and you will experience me as Illuminating Bliss. See how fragile this loving intimacy is. It can only happen in tender vulnerability, in surrendering to Eternal Love, in complete nakedness.*"

§ 25. The Twins - Gemini

♊ ☿

When Idris speaks these words, the scene shifts, and I arrive in a garden. Instead of the Sun, the Moon and the Stars I see a naked man who is looking at a naked woman.

"These are the Cosmic Twins, Heru. They are Soul Mates, described in so many books. But never look for them outside of yourself, they are a part of you. He is Orpheus looking for his lost Euridice. She is the widow Isis, on her eternal search throughout the Universe for her deceased husband Osiris. He is Dante following the voice of Beatrice in search for Paradise. You can find these two lovers in the great myths of the Earth. Because they are so important you will find them between the stars of the Zodiac as the constellation Gemini. And there is one more mystery. The Sun and the Moon united you already know in form of the hieroglyph for the constellation of Taurus – ♉. But connected to Gemini is the planet Mercury, the planet of Inner Plane Communication. Underneath the Sun and Moon, you will find the Cross of the Elements -☿.That is my sign, by this sign you will recognize me."

§ 26. The Soul of Light

"Look at your Cosmic Parents, Heru, they are the two Pillars of Creation. They are your Cosmic Father and your Cosmic Mother. Through their unification they created you: the Soul of Light. When the Sword of Eternal Love comes down from heaven, it connects

male and female energies in a lightning flash. In this way the Sword not only divides, but also becomes the Light of Ecstasy that balances and connects the powers of polarity. When the Lightning Flash reaches the Earth, it becomes the Sword in the Stone."

"Solve et Coagula, separate and unify: that is the Law of the Cosmos. That eternal movement causes the entire Universe to come into existence. Look above, Heru, look at the place from whence you came". And I look into the direction of the Voice, and see Eros appearing in the light of the setting sun. The surrealistic light slowly makes place for a night sky sparked with stars. A distant mountain reaches up towards the heavens.
"Pay attention, because you will be witnessing another mystery," Eros speaks, "*Watch how the Star Goddess comes down to unite with the Earth god"*.

I see how the Goddess stretches out her arms across the landscape and how she takes her seat and encloses the mountain and takes him into her starry body. *"What will come forth from this unification?" I ask* the Voice.
"The Goddess will give birth to new stars", Eros answers. "*The stars will hold the essences of all that was, that is, and that will be"*.

§ 27. The Two Trees

I notice how the arms of the Star Goddess solidify: at the place where she has touched the ground two trees start to grow. In one tree four pomegranates are hanging. In the other tree twelve fire flowers bloom.

"It is important to mark this point, Heru. The entrance to the Enchanted World can be found between the Two Trees of the Star Goddess. You need to know this spot to find the Way Back. If you try to travel into the Otherworld and ignore this entrance, you will arrive in a realm of complete chaos. There is no light there and no redemption. But if you take the road in between these two Trees, you will find guides, angels and gods who will show you the way."

"*What is so special about these trees?*" I ask.

"The first tree holds pomegranates; it is the Tree of the Knowledge of Good and Evil. This tree contains the Wisdom of Transformation through the senses. You will climb this tree on the back of the Serpent of Desire. It is important that you balance your desires, use your virtues and work at your vices. The serpent is the Guardian of the Sacred Garden, through her you will collect wisdom, and she will give you fuel for your transformation."

"I see four pomegranates hanging in the tree, but we have five senses, don't we?" I wonder.

"I gave you the fifth pomegranate at the beginning of this road, Heru, it materialized as your physical body. Now look at the other tree, this is the legendary Burning Bush. When

the Tree of Life develops to its fullest potential, all its Sephiroth change into Sapphires, and between the leaves of the Tree starflowers start to burn brightly; they are the Powers of the Zodiac brought to perfection."

§ 28. Mountain of Sunset

"When you pass the Two Trees you arrive at the Road towards the Mount of Salvation. Walk this road, Heru, it will bring you to the Inner Garden. I as the Guardian of the Sacred Mountain will open the way for you when the time is right. For now, the clouds will veil this eternal wisdom for you."

§ 29. Eros

"Now I will tell you something about myself, Heru. Do not confuse me with sexual desire, that is merely a part of me. Do not confuse me with Cupid, sexual power. I am a far older god, one of the first gods who came into existence. I am the Son of the Night, the God of Graceful Love, the Firstborn Son of the Universe and the Goddess of the Night, the Beloved One of Psyche. I am an eagle that soars on the winds and a jackal that shows the way through the desert. I come forth from the Void, I cross the Abyss. I am the guardian who guards the path that connects pure consciousness with the Chapel of the Heart. My voice will lead you to this sacred place. You will get there when you sort out the seeds of your psyche."

§ 30. Meditation: The Hieros Gamos

Unite the Sun and the Moon and find your Inner Lover,
Follow the Voice of the Winds
Discover the Beloved One of Psyche,
And experience the Hieros Gamos at the Chapel of the Heart.

"I have a gift for you, Heru, I will give you a magical potion. If you drink one sip, you will be able to contact your Inner Lover. The rest of the potion is for people you meet who need it. It has great healing capacities."

Then the Doors to the Great Hall swing open, the nebula drift apart and I step into the Hall of the Mountain King, with the black and white tiled floor and the stained-glass doors. The situation of the Wounded King remains unchanged. Many healers have been visiting him since I saw him the last time, but the deep wound in his groins is still bleeding. I greet him, and assure him that I will do my utmost to find a solution. I tell him what I have discovered so far: *"Dear King, I have met my Inner Lover. I did not know that Love can go so deep. There is no betrayal possible if one falls in love with one's twin soul; I have learned that my twin soul is a part of myself that stayed behind in Heaven, when I was born on Earth. The Inner Lover is a gift from Eros for the true seeker. Eros has granted me a magical potion. It will enable you to contact your Inner Lover, too. I will offer you a sip of this magical potion,"* and I bend over to the King, and help him take a sip from the bottle. Then I cork the bottle again, sighing. Slowly I rise and store the bottle with the love potion in the pouch on my Batocchio.

Now Idris interferes: *"You have done extremely well, Heru. But for now, it is time to return to the profane world, and contemplate the deep truths that have been communicated to you on the Inner Planes. Everything needs to be digested. Tap with your wand while you repeat the spell and you will return to your own world, into the Here-and-Now."*

I follow Idris' directions and I tap three times with my wand on the floor. I feel how the waters enclose me again, and I tumble downwards into the waterfall. Everywhere around me I see the mists closing in. I become aware of my physical surroundings. I feel my body, I stretch my muscles while I repeat the spell, I wake up in the physical world, feeling great.

The Catch Exercise is an exercise that you take with you into your profane life. The catch exercise which belongs to this tarot card consists of searching inside at odd moments and listening to the voice of your Inner Lover. Make notes of what it communicates to you.

The Contemplation Exercise is a waking meditation, a pondering over a philosophical concept. You can do it with a good glass of wine next to a fireplace. The story about the Lovers is full of philosophical concepts. Contemplate the different concepts and symbolic representations in the story line.

*****

The Golden Ring in Spring

If you want to learn more about the myths belonging to these three tarot cards, look at the website. In the shop you will find several programs to deepen your knowledge even more:

https://www.hermeticartsandsciences.org/product/video-course-the-golden-ring-in-spring-tarot-journey-2/

The Enchanting Spring of Gorias, and the Tapestries of the Goddess in Aries, Taurus and Gemini are forthcoming.

VII ♋ THE BOAT OF HEAVEN ה

Trump VII – Cancer

The Boat of Heaven

The Child of the Powers of the Waters

Hebrew letter	**Cheth ח meaning Fence, Enclosure**
Simple Letter	**Speech**
Path color	**Red-Orange**
Sign	**Cancer ♋**

Thirty-Two Paths of Wisdom:

The Eighteenth Path is called the House of Influence (by the greatness of whose abundance the influx of good things upon created beings is increased), and from the midst of the investigation the arcane and hidden senses are drawn forth, which dwell in its shade and which cling to it, from the cause of all causes.

After dealing with issues of the mundane world for a while, I feel an urge to visit the Inner Worlds again. I strongly feel that it is time to take the next journey to the Hall of the Mountain King. I clear my calendar of my obligations and withdraw into my meditation room. There I take my Batocchio in my hand and I repeat the spell that Idris taught me: I visualize the Double Doors in front of me. I tap three times with the Batocchio on the floor and whisper:

Now do I descend into the Inner Seas
Whose Waters rise and fall within my soul
Now let the Inner Elements be seduced and still
Let me immerse myself into those Living Waters
And emerging therefrom
Let me bring from latent stress to potent image
The symbol of the King's High Table

In wonder I witness how a nebula appears in the center of the Hall of the Mountain King, and solidifies. It takes the form of the great lapis lazuli Round Table. I watch this phenomenon taking place in amazement, the more I concentrate on the manifestation, the more solid the Table becomes. When the Table is fully manifested, Idris appears in his own magical way. A second nebula appears in the hall and miraculously the bearded Mage condensates. When he is fully manifested, Idris taps with his wand on the floor and speaks: *"As the Sun moves through the seasons, it illuminates the glass doors one by one. The last time you visited the hall it was the season of Gemini. But now the Sun is approaching Summer. Watch how the Doors to Cancer open."*

I watch how the Sun moves on the outside of the hall and see how the stained-glass door of Cancer becomes illuminated, and a new part of the broad golden band forms that connects the doors of Gemini and Cancer. I clearly see the representation of a charioteer on the stained glass now. Idris gestures that I have to tap with my Batocchio. I hear a clear clicking sound when the stained-glass doors unlock and reveal the entrance to the next Cave. Immediately I feel all the physical sensations of the shift between the worlds. I am very curious what the nature of reality will be in the next Cave I am allowed to visit.

§ 31. The White City

The Voice of Idris fades away, the only sound that remains, is the sound of rushing waves. I look around where this noise is coming from, and I notice that I have arrived in a harbor on the edge of a vast endless ocean. All around me I see the starry night sky, above and below in a reflection of exalted beauty. In the harbor a lonely reed boat is floating. Its prow is beautifully shaped in the form of a sea dragon. Vaguely I can see some strangely formed objects on the boat.

From the mists that hover over the waters, a strange figure steps forward. The creature is clad in sheepskin. It is not very tall, it hardly reaches my shoulder. It is neither male nor female. When it comes closer, I see that the figure is holding an earthenware pot. I step forward and look into its eyes and then I ask the creature: "*Who are you?*"

The creature bows. *"I have come to guide you on your next journey, Heru, my name is Kurgarra. I am created by the highest God. From the dirt he had under his fingernail he created me. He fed me with the Food of Life and offered me a drink from the Water of Life. Then I was shown the way into the Underworld. I know of the journey that lies ahead of you and I can teach you how to use the secret powers that are connected to the gifts which are stored in the reed boat."*

Kurgarra steps onto the reed boat and indicates for me to follow him. I have to move carefully to not disturb the fragile balance of the boat. I balance my weight by holding on tightly to the railing. I look around and observe the strange objects that are gathered here. Kurgarra walks directly towards the mast of the boat and points at the skin of a corpse that hangs there on a nail: *"I went to the Underworld to collect the corpse that hung from a nail on the wall, in the deepest Cave of the Underworld Goddess. This corpse belongs to the Goddess Inanna."*

Then Kurgarra takes his jar and starts to sprinkles the fluid inside onto the corpse and me... while he mumbles strange words... . Then I become aware that the mists start to envelop me and I am being enclosed in a vortex of light and winds. The winds quickly increase in power and I become surrounded by rushing rains and howling hurricanes: I am in the middle of a raging thunderstorm, I am in the center of thunder, lightning and torrential rain. A lightning flash breaks through the pitch-black clouds and I feel that I am hit! I am in the center of the lightning storm, I feel I am drawn into the corpse... and I arise as Inanna...

§ 32. Inanna

... and I hear the voice of Kurgarra when he shouts: *"Inanna, Lady of all the magical powers, Resplendent Light, righteous woman clothed in radiance, beloved by the Gods! Mistress of Heaven, with the great magical jewels, High Priestess of Heaven, who wields all seven of the magical powers! My lady, you are the guardian of those great creative powers! Take up your might, hang your magical jewelry into your ears, around your neck, onto your hands, hang them over your breast. Come to life again, wake up and drink from the waters of the Well of Knowledge! Learn to use your gifts - the Holy Me - that you have received from the Gods!"*

And I feel how my consciousness expands and rises ... and I enter into a State of Grace! I become embedded in that Bliss, which is the gift of the pitch-black darkened ocean that is called The Great Sea. My vision shifts and I am taken back into the Deep, into the Far Past where the memories of the planet are stored in the Great Cloud of Knowledge while I merge with Inanna.

I know that I have just visited my father Enki. He has given me great magical gifts: they are called the *Sacred Me's*. I have stored all these beautiful treasures in my reed boat. The Me's are treasures that hold great magical potency. With these sacred objects I am capable of wielding the Seven Magical Powers!

I try out my Seat of Power: I sit down on the mighty Lapis Lazuli Throne that stands in the center of my ship between four poles. Then I take the Wand of Power into my hands. After feeling its weight and powers, I put it on a special stand. I feel the presence of the Seven Magical Powers hovering around me.

On the other side of the throne the Lamp of Venus hangs. The light in the lamp burns brightly in the form of an eight-pointed star. With this lamp, I will be able to measure the length of the year.

But the most important object in the reed boat, is the nut from the Tree of Life. I will plant this nut as soon as I arrive in the Netherworld, and it will grow into a big tree. It will grant me the Worship of the people, the praying and the kneeling and the prostrating. I will water it with holy water.

Aboard the ship I admire my treasures and I make myself beautiful. I kneel down and look into the treasure box to see what is in there: I find a strangely shaped headdress. Carefully I put the Horned Crown on my head. I also find the Claws of an Eagle: I put them on my feet and on my back, I fasten its wings.

My father has given to me costly and powerful jewels. In the treasure box I find the Jewels of Sound. I hang those beautiful earrings into my ears and I now hear the sounds of birds, the rushing waters of streams and the first cry of newly born animals. I hang the Necklace of Spells around my neck and my voice calls upon all the Magical Powers of the Words of Creation that can build a World and destroy it... I put my Bracelets of Power around my wrists and when I raise my arms. I call up the Seven Powers of Space, my heart starts to beat with ecstasy, and I become ecstatic with all the rising juices of spring, I dance and mate, together with all the animals. Around my waist I tie the Belt of Dance. It gives me beauty, sex appeal and the rhythm of music. I put the Bells of Joy onto my fingers and pick up the instrument that lies at the bottom of the chest. My fingers move over the strings of the Harp of Lamentation: now I am the Singer of Sorrows. I create the Song of Darkness; I sing the Songs of Fate and the Songs of Sighs. *"Look, Kurgarra, I am dressed in a Garment of Light!"*

Kurgarra bows deeply, he prostrates and answers with a trembling voice: *"Clothed in Radiance and dressed in Resplendent Light, my queen, you are the Unfailing Woman, wearing brilliance, Queen of the Fundamental Forces, crowned with Goodness."*

"Kurgarra, we are ready for our journey. Push this Ship off the shore, into the Great Deep. I will raise a huge tidal wave that will bring us to the Enchanted Garden. Let us sail across the River of Lights and absorb all its Powers!"
When I have done that, I shout out joyfully: *"I am Inanna and I bring down the Sacred Me's!"*

§ 33. The Journey to the Great Below

Now Kurgarra loses the rope that ties the reed boat to the shore and pushes us away. My journey into the unknown has begun. I sail over the River of Fire. The pitch-black night sky changes its colors into Lapis Lazuli blue and it is speckled with golden lights. The Night condenses into a beautiful transparent garment; a veil of blue light and golden beauty covers the Enchanted Lands and thus divides Eternity from the World of Time. I decide to take the veil with me into the reed boat. I turn it into a baldachin, a canopy for my Lapis Lazuli Throne. While I'm doing this, I realize that I wield the Powers of Creation. I translate my spiritual purpose into form and motion.

The boat moves and the waters are rough. The rapids pull me in every direction. I realize that I need to learn how to steer the boat. While I am wondering how to solve this problem Kurgarra speaks: "*Inanna, you need to get control over the sea horses! In this moment they pull the reed boat into two different directions.*"

I look around if I can find reins to steer them. But there are no leather belts or ropes of any kind aboard the ship: *"Kurgarra, my guide, how do I steer my reed boat and give direction to the sea horses?"*

"My lady, the sea horses are the embodiment of the Powers of Polarity. They come into being as soon as Creation manifests from No-thingness. Without polarity creation is not possible. The only way to direct polarity is by making use of Wisdom and of Willpower; they will be your reins."

And the journey continues while I direct my mind, and steer the sea horses into the direction of the Great Below. We journey from the Great Sea across the River of Fire, into the World of Manifestation. We cross an Abyss filled with spiritual force that condenses in archetypical forms while we pass. It is an amazing sight to watch Gods and Giants, Angels and Elves come into being, to see Ideas and Principles taking shape.

§ 34. The Boat

Suddenly I realize that also the boat itself is alive. I realize that everything that is created is born from seafoam. Everything takes shape through the power of Thought and through the Word. The power to give words to ideas creates the Sacred Art of the Mastery of Thought. As soon as a Spiritual Essence is realized and given a Thoughtform and a name, it starts to manifest! It does not matter whether it is Inanna and Kurgarra, or the reed boat and the sea horses. In that Supreme Dark Abyss we are crossing, I discover my inner senses and the Power to Create: I have created a reed boat! I have created four pillars that hold up a baldachin of stars! I have created the two sea horses named Wisdom and Willpower to steer the ship. The boat is movement: it is the vehicle of the Spirit and carries within itself all the archetypes to manifest Spirit. On the boat they manifest in form of costumes. One garment for each level of existence, for every world we will visit on our journey... And when I realize all of this, I feel all my Powers and Talents exploding in an exaltation of pure joy! My conquest is on all the planes. I steer all the forces of creation; I am exalted above all things, triumphant in mind!

I notice that we are now entering into the world of manifestation, where I will create the external world. In order to do that effectively my powers to manifest must get a shape as well. It is important that, when the beautiful and vulnerable spiritual forces manifest, they need to become clothed in a strong outward shell. As a token for this principle, I put the Sign of Cancer on the Baldachin of Stars. After I have done that, I shout out joyfully: *"I am Inanna and I bring down the Sacred Me's!"*

§ 35. The Magical Garden

I have now left the River of Fires in the Night, and I have passed the River of Stars by Day. I notice that - when I sail through the Double Doors that separate Eternity from Time - the boat slides through them exactly at the time of the Summer Solstice.

Kurgarra tells me: "*We are right on time. This is exactly the right moment to create the Road of Initiation into Humanity! You have exactly the right magical instruments aboard that will bring this task about. Let us step ashore and plant the Tree of Life!*"

The reed boat moors ashore and I step on dry land. With my bare hands, I dig a hole into the ground. Then I take the nut of the Tree and carefully place it in the mud. *"Kurgarra, I need the Fluid of Life that is in your jar!"*

While Kurgarra starts to water the nut of the Tree, I tell him: *"In the center of my Magical Garden there is a secret place. It is the most holy place in the world because it contains the Cauldron of Creation. Let me concentrate to bring about the Miracles that it keeps inside."*

Then I direct all my powers to that place within, where the Forces of Creation form the Chalice of Life. I take these creative powers in my hands. I notice that the Chalice of Life is filled with the Life Force and the Holy Blood. Once again, I call down the Powers of the Lightning Flash, while I stir the Sacred Blood with my Horn of Abundance and thus, I create the First Vortex, the Power of Magic: *"Kurgarra, watch how I keep stirring the mixture. I will spin an essence into being with the Energy of Creation. With every stir and with every magical word I speak, I conjure up the forces that generate this light! With the first vortex I gather all the forces and I create a Fountain of Light. Its forces clothe everything I manifest in a Garment of Beauty."*

Through the second vortex my Tree starts to grow roots that form all the Powers of the Underworld. Its leaves generate all the Powers of the Upper World and its trunk will create the manifested world, wherein I will create my residence. In this way I create the manifestation of the Greatest Good and the Wonder of Mysteries."

"In making use of the third vortex, watch how a point of light forms, right in the center of the Cauldron. It is the Flame of the Soul of every living being. It grows from individual to tribal, to global and universal. Watch how this Sacred Fluid now starts to give form to all the forces of humanity, all its foolishness and wisdom, all its powers of destruction and growth, its life and its death... See the great Mystery is taking place, watch how the Earth becomes filled with all its life forms: with plants, with birds in the sky and fishes in the sea, with animals to walk the earth, and with humanity: all are created by the Magic of Thoughtforms and the Fluid of Life. We all are born from the Cauldron of Creation..."

In Beauty, Wonder and Mystery

When my work is almost finished, I wield my Staff of Power and I ignite the solar flame. I make a full circle and inscribe a river of light around the Earth; the ecliptic path of the Sun:

"Every living being will be able to watch my Boat of Light sail on this River of Gold. With my golden boat I will encircle my Sacred Garden. My boat is the Sun, but it is guided by Kurgarra, whose essence is the subconscious Power of the Moon. I name this River of Gold Cheth, because it is both a path and a fence, to protect my Magical Garden. In this way my Inner Garden can be safely cultivated. I will call this Garden PRDS – Paradise - and give it the title 'The House of Influence'. When I have done that, I shout out joyfully: 'I am Inanna and I bring down the Sacred Me's!'"

Then I feel a shift in consciousness again. The overshadowing of Inanna leaves me, and I become aware of my own identity again; I am an ordinary fool caught up in an adventure. And I realize my true essence:

§ 36. Meditation: P R D S

I am Heru,
The Power that grows the Sacred Garden of the Soul
I clothe all the Forces of the Spirit
In a Garment of Thought and Speech
So that they manifest.

Now Idris approaches me again: *"Realize that you have been given an immensely important gift, Heru, the power to create your Magical Garden. This is a protected area in your Inner World. In this garden you can sow the seeds of virtues and talents. If you take good care of this garden, your Inner Life will grow and blossom as well as your profane life. Take your pouch from your Batocchio, Heru. Take out the four stones that Eternity gave you when you descended."*

I do that and I discover four stones that have strange signs written on them:

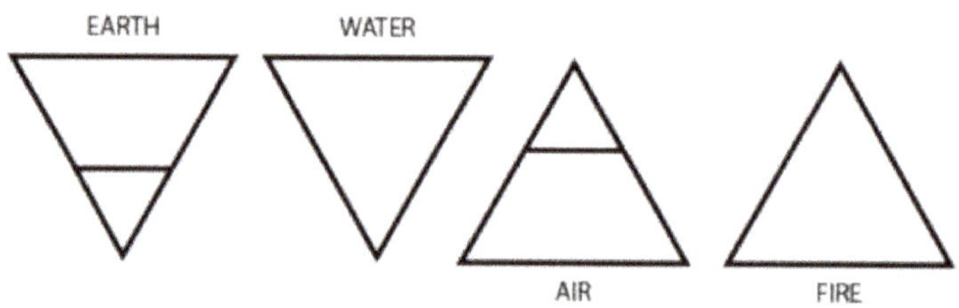

"Sow these stones into your magical garden to mark the directions and the borders. The Stone of Air goes into the North, the stone of Earth goes into the East, the Stone of Fire you need to plant in the South, and the Stone of Water in the West. The most important thing of all is that your Enchanted Lands are large enough, and that the Mountain of Salvation and the Castle of the King are located exactly in the center. Now step into your Sacred Garden, and assume your position in the center of the garden, in front of the entrance of the Castle. Look towards the four cardinal directions, and then slowly turn around and see your Magical Garden unfold:

- In the North, the Enchanted Lands are called Falias. Here it is as dark as the night. You look at a winter landscape where a blizzard dresses the scenery in a mantle of snow.

- In the East, the Sun is rising over the Lands of Gorias, as a new dawn and the leaves of the plants and their flowers unfold in anticipation of a spring day.

- In the South, you oversee a dusty summer landscape, here are the Lands of Findias. Vine branches grow on the slopes. They stand in rows, their branches gently touching each other. They look like dancers holding hands, ready for a round dance. Further away, the slopes are planted with succulents and cacti. In the distance, you see a spewing volcano.

- In the West, the Sun is setting over the Lands of Murias. The sky slowly deepens, its colors from azure into cobalt blue and the clouds change from white to yellow, orange and purple. In this spectacular display of colors, the Moon rises above an endless ocean. Foaming waves rush ashore. The dune forests are adorned with yellow red foliage and show you that autumn rules here.

"Your task for the coming time is to internalize your Enchanted Lands. Use your wand and draw an imaginative circle at the height of your navel. Then you repeat the spell that you have learned:

I am Heru,
The Power that grows the Sacred Garden of the Soul
I clothe all the Forces of the Spirit
In a Garment of Thought and Speech
So that they manifest.

Look into each of the cardinal directions, and visualize the Magical Landscape in as much detail as you can. Internalize this image, so that you can dream of it.

Then the doors to the Hall of the Mountain King swing open, the nebula drift apart and I step into the Great Hall with the black and white tiled floor and the stained-glass doors. The Wounded King is still moaning on his bed. Nothing has changed for him. Many healers have been visiting him since I visited him the last time, but the deep wound in his groins is still bleeding. I greet him and assure him that I will do my utmost to find a solution. I tell him what I have discovered so far: *"Dear King, this time I am coming to bring you the secret of the Enchanted Lands. I have sown the stones of the Cardinal Directions, created a Magical Paradise Garden and freed the soil from weed. In my garden I have planted the nut of the Tree of Life. I have watered my garden thoroughly, so I assume that everything I sow will start to grow and blossom. As soon as I can harvest the first fruits from the Enchanted Lands, I will bring them to you."*

The King answers: *"You have done a wonderful job, Heru. But for now, it is time for you to return to the profane world."*

I nod my head and walk to the place at the Round Table where my Zodiac sign is inscribed. There I tap three times with my wand on the floor. I feel how the mists enclose me again. I become aware of my physical surroundings. I feel my body, I stretch my muscles while I repeat the spell, I wake up in the physical world, feeling great.

XI ♌ THE LEADER OF THE LION ט

Trump XI – Leo ♌

The Leader of the Lion

Strength

Hebrew letter Teth ט
Simple Letter
Path color yellow gold
Sign Leo ♌

Thirty-Two Paths of Wisdom:

The Nineteenth Path is the Intelligence of all the activities and spiritual beings, and it is so called because of the affluence diffused by it from the most high blessing and most exalted sublime glory.

§ 37. The Cave of the Leader of the Lion

After the boat trip into the Cave of the Boat of Heaven, I take care of my garden. It is a lot of work to weed out the unwanted herbs. I dig the soil, and every day I water the nut of the Tree of Life, and I see its shoot emerging from the ground.

I am very proud of how barren soil slowly changes into fertile ground. Before I continue planting my garden I long to explore the Four Countries of the Enchanted Lands and all the different realities that are somehow linked to the Enchanted Castle. I start to feel the urge to take the next journey to the Hall of the Mountain king, and I long to hear from the King how he is doing after my previous magical gift. I take my Batocchio in my hand and repeat the spell that Idris taught me. I visualize the Double Doors in front of me. I tap three times with the wand on the floor and whisper:

Now do I descend into the Inner Seas
Whose Waters rise and fall within my soul
Now let the Inner Elements be seduced and still
Let me immerse myself into those Living Waters
And emerging therefrom
Let me bring from latent stress to potent image
The symbol of the King's High Table

I arrive in the now familiar Hall of the Mountain King. I greet the King, his situation is still unchanged, or maybe he has even weakened a little bit. His voice trembles as he assures me how welcome I am in his hall and his palace.
I ask the King: *"Does the pain get worse because of the weight your responsibility? Is your pain not dulled by the weight of the crown?"*
The Wounded King answers: *"A crown brings burdens of its own kind – in each throb of my side echo the cries of my people."*

Then I watch how in the center of the Great Hall a nebula appears, and it solidifies in the form of the great lapis lazuli blue Round Table. Immediately after my arrival Idris appears in his own unique way. The Hall fills itself with unmistakably magical energy and the Mage materializes in the center of the Hall. When he is fully manifested, Idris speaks: *"On its journey around the cycle of the year, the Sun moves through the seasons, and it illuminates the glass doors one by one. The last time you visited the hall it was the season of Cancer. But now it is becoming high Summer. Let us witness how the Doors to Leo open, we will visit the Cave of the Leader of the Lion."*

I watch the Sun moving outside the hall and see how the stained-glass door of Leo becomes illuminated, and a new part of the broad golden band forms and connects the doors of Cancer and Leo. I can now clearly see the depiction of a Goddess riding a lioness on the stained glass. Idris gestures with his wand and says; *"Behold, the Leader of the Lion."*

I am very curious what the nature of reality will be in the next Cave I am allowed to visit. Then Idris indicates that I have to tap with my Batocchio. And immediately I feel all the physical sensations of the shift between the worlds.

When my wand taps on the floor for the first time, I see how the entire scene begins to whirl before my eyes, the colors merge and I feel a strange shiver running through my whole body. With the next tap, all the images that I see - both with my physical eyes and in my head – are lifted into the air! It is as if these images are leaves that fly on the wind, they whirl around in a vortex of color. With the third tap I feel myself being pulled into this vortex of powers. My heart is beating with a mixture of excitement and fear. I ask myself, what did I get myself into? Everything around me becomes volatile and fluid, except for one thing: everywhere around me glittering shards fall from the sky. I am surrounded by a shower of falling glittering shards of a mirror that rains down from Heaven. All around me I hear the sound of breaking glass. I become disoriented. I hear the sharp tinkling noise of glass falling on the floor. Between the falling glass, a card from a tarot deck floats downwards. It falls upside down on one of the shards. *"Pick it up and take it with you,"* Idris remarks.
I bend over to pick up the shard and tuck it away in my pouch. Then I hear the characteristic noise when the stained-glass door opens. Idris and I step through the door and witness a strange scene coming to life!

At first, everything turns pitch black. I notice that the flame of my lantern struggles to stay alive, a tiny blue flame gasps for fuel. Then Idris steps forward from the void. He picks up my lantern. In Idris' hands, the flame immediately comes to life again and I can see what is going on around me.

We enter a strange room. In the room there stands a cubical altar with a black obsidian mirror on a stand on top. Idris steps towards the altar and swings the lantern over the obsidian mirror three times. I now clearly see the sun reflected in it. But instead of the bright golden daystar, the black mirror shows a solar eclipse. From the obsidian glass a surrealistic light radiates. Its magical energy fills the room and I witness a frozen scene slowly coming to life.

I am in a chamber where all the walls are covered in pure gold. There is a mosaic on the floor, made of black and golden stones, it depicts a labyrinth. On both sides of the altar there are two marble statues: a female and a male figure, each seated on a throne. They are clad in hooded robes. Both figures wear masks. Behind the two statues a banner flies with seven sigils. On the altar, next to the obsidian mirror a papyrus scroll lies, sealed with seven seals. I am really curious and step forward to take a closer look. Idris holds me back. He looks at me with an intense gaze: *"Be careful Heru. This is a magical Cave. A Cave like the ones Eternity told you about. This is a frozen scene. If anything, that is represented here resonates within you, if you get emotionally involved, you will be drawn into the adventure and you will have to live through it!"*

I know, I know... I am nosy, it got me into trouble before! I feel attracted to the statues and I step forward, in spite of Idris's warning. I see movement in the left statue and watch it come to life! It shakes its muscles, rises and the female figure removes her mask.

"Too late", Idris sighs. *"Heru, you meet Inanna again, but now in a darker aspect. In this Cave the Queen of Heaven appears in her office of Leader of the Lion."*

The lady now removes the hooded cape. She shakes her long curly hair. Inanna is an impressing figure. She is as beautiful as the Living Daylight! She has long yellow hair that resembles the sun. She wears a necklace of carnelian rosettes around her holy neck: in the center of the biggest stone, the hieroglyph for Leo ♌ is engraved. Inanna wears a lion skin. She holds a caduceus wand with two living snakes in her right hand and a sickle knife in her left hand.

While I am taking in what happens, Idris explains the nature of this Cave: "*Inanna is a very powerful goddess who was already worshipped in Sumer at 4000 BCE. When you meet the oldest gods, you must know that they are not human beings, but personalized natural forces. By personalizing them, you can build a relationship and interact with them at any moment, day or night. You can recognize them everywhere around you. Divinity is not something distant, spirituality is not an escapism from the world. The oldest gods are no 'merry and meek' beings, but vast and often fearsome powers."*

The name of this Sacred Cave is the Leader of the Lion. It is a teaching Cave. It teaches you the 'intelligence of all the activities and spiritual beings.' The method of the teaching is: experiencing and controlling all aspects of yourself."

By this time Inanna has shaken off every characteristic of a statue and I stand face to face with a large powerful goddess, from whose appearance an awesome glow of dignity radiates. Then I hear her voice for the first time. It reminds me of thunder and lightning, it sounds like the roaring voice of a lioness: *"Welcome Heru, into my Cave of Courage. I am Inanna. I am the Earth herself; the Bride of a powerful King. Whenever you meet me on Earth, you can recognize me by my robe of pure daylight. Whenever I travel through the Heavens, I am clothed in my raw powers. Whenever I travel through the Underworld, I am invisible. But wherever I am, I wear my mantle of brilliance and light."*

While pondering what Inanna tells me, I wonder: if she is the brilliance of the Earth, who will be her king? I have hardly finished that thought when the next statue starts to come alive. The male figure bends over and reaches with his hand into my pouch. He pulls out the shard of the Mirror of Heaven with the tarot card depicted on it and rises up. He turns the card around and shows the image of the Leader of the Lion to me. Then he takes off his mask. Before I can see his face, he replaces the mask with the glittering shard and I look into my own face. Immediately I sense the pulling force of the vortex again and feel how I am drawn into the statue of the king. I merge with the king; I am the King.

Now Idris steps forward to the altar and lifts his arms up to the sky. I watch the clouds constrict and create a formation of blackness. A lightning flash hits Inanna's Caduceus wand. As the lightning bolt strikes the staff, the entire mountain shakes, the castle rattles and all the surrounding lands shudder. I watch how the two snakes come to life. They wind themselves around the staff.

Idris speaks again. His breath equals the whirling winds. His voice echoes from all around me: *"I notice that your sovereignty is challenged: Heru, are you the rightful king? Your throne is unstable! Why is that so? Did you abuse your power? Or are you a righteous king and is evil threatening you, I see you are wounded? Heru, on this path the Sword of the God of Matter is forged. You need to be able to use it when necessary. But with such a powerful weapon to restore the balance in your hands, you need to be able to control those powers: take care that you do not become overwhelmed by them!"*

I contemplate my own situation and the personal challenges in my life that keep me busy. I truly ask myself the question: "*Is it me who causes all these problems in my life? Is it a character flaw of mine, a blind spot, a form of naivety? Or is this upheaval caused by King Herla? King Herla... Where did he go after the Descent? Then I ask myself where King Herla is at this moment? And I ask Idris: "What happened to King Herla?"*

Idris sighs: *"This is not a nice story, Heru. After King Herla caused the Fall, he continued on his journey. It was he who destroyed the Star Mirror in the sky, that same mirror you saw falling down. After committing these crimes, he drove downwards. He split the surface of the Earth and established his kingdom in the deepest parts of the Inner Earth. There he proclaimed himself to be King over the Forces of Chaos. From this dark place he rules the Forces of Mischief. Heru, if you want to become king over your own Inner Kingdom, you need to face the machinations of King Herla. You need to gain rulership over the Forces of Chaos. You will have to battle King Herla and his army of destructive forces. In order to win this battle, you will need the courage and the power to control and tame a lioness!"*

Now Idris raises his arms to the heavens and lifts his staff a second time. The dragon, carved from gemstone, which sits on top of his staff comes to life. His eyes flash, his wings move, his tail curls around the wood. I feel the powers of magic whirling around me again. I hear the voice of Idris echoing and filling the entire Inner Landscape: *"Let the invisible become visible!"*

Everything around me shakes, and I feel my body change. My arms and legs change into paws with claws. My skull expands and I grow a mane. I feel how I shapeshift into a lion. I start to radiate light as if I were the Sun itself. I feel how my powers increase. My muscles grow stronger. My teeth grow larger; I get powerful jaws and I rrroarrr!

My heart swells. It grows, becomes extremely big and bright and starts to shine like a star in the night. Now Idris bends over to me and instructs me regarding to the coming challenges: "*You have activated the Cave of Courage, Heru. This is an area where your strength is challenged. The Inner Work of the Cave of Courage is to face everything that happens to you from the inside, to take responsibility for it and transform it. Nothing can be refused, because if you did, you would deny a part of yourself and this would violate the Law of Love. The Lioness rules in all the Worlds. In this Cave, you meet Inanna as the Underworld Goddess of the South; she guards the entrance to the realm where your courage will be tested. Are you prepared, are you ready to meet her?*"

"Descend into your Underworld, Heru. The Realm of the Subconscious Mind has seven layers. Every layer is a level of awareness of the Deep Mind. Every layer gives you access to regions of chaotic forces. In this underworldly realm, the King Herla's Army of Mischief obstructs your Self. The only way to win this battle is through courage and ethics."

"You are not allowed to kill your opponents, because in killing him you would kill a part of yourself. In order to win this battle, you need to transform them so that they become helpful forces, which cause personal growth. Work with everything that happens to you during your life. Use every experience for your personal evolution and transformation. Your lion-essence embodies the raw forces of nature of the subjective world. Through your work they will gradually grow into their highest essence."

"The first step is to learn how to work with the different stages of Alchemical Fire. If you get this fire under the conscious control of your Inner Sun, you will get access to levels of illumination of consciousness beyond the Sphere of the Sun: the Superconscious Realm. You will merge with the highest light. If your integrity, your strength and your courage have grown strong enough, you will be able to open the Seven Seals of the Scroll of Heaven," Idris says, pointing at the scroll on the altar.

"Behold, the Sacred Scroll of the Apocalypse. It lies on the altar in this Sacred Cave. Are you strong and courageous enough to open the scroll and look at its contents? Behold, when you break the Seven Seals, the battle of the Underworld against the machinations of King Herla will begin. If you win, the forces involved will change and transform into magical powers."

Then Inanna climbs on my back. She lifts the Caduceus Wand. I see the two snakes curling around it, climbing upwards in a love dance to reach the pineapple on top... I hear her voice again: *"Behold, the symbol of Spinal Fire. The snakes around my wand of power symbolize the neurological network around your spine; the pineapple depicts the pituitary gland in your brain."*

Now she lifts her necklace and shows me the stone with the sign for Leo ♌ on it. Then she takes one of her serpents from the staff, wraps it around me...

§ 38. She who tames the Lion

Inanna spurs me as if I were a horse that she rides. I have to run at full speed with the powerful goddess on my back. We gallop through all kinds of landscapes and weather patterns. We cross all the seasons. We travel through old scenes: I see memories, trauma's, happy events that lifted my life. Then the Goddess starts to explain what she is up to:

The Green Lion

"Let me tell you about the stages of the transformation of the Lion. Your first transformation takes place when you recognize the lion-essence in yourself and become able to identify with it. This is where you are right now, Heru. You are a Green Lion. Your decisions are driven by that raw natural animal energy, the instincts before any willpower has been gained; pure natural animal instincts. In this Cave you need to learn how to control them and to become a master over your sexual powers."

The Red Lion

As soon as you are able to bring these inner natural forces under perfect control, you will transform into a Red Lion. As a Red Lion you learn to use karmic and spiritual energy to transform your sexual drive into a power that enables you to access higher levels of consciousness."

Regulus

"When this transformation has been fully achieved, you will have developed a spiritual level where your soul gives off so much light that this stage is called the Golden Child. Then you will merge with the Heavenly Lion, with the Heart of the Lion – the star Regulus. Its name means the King, the Mighty, the Centre. In the Heart of the Lion the development of Inner Kingship begins. Regulus brings peace, civilization and gives laws to the country and the people. In your Inner Kingdom you will develop structure and order. All the parts of the Soul of Light will start to work together harmoniously. This process is called Healing the Wounded King. When the King and the Queen mate, they heal the wounded King. Heru, realize that the Hieros Gamos starts in the Underworld. "

Inanna continues and explains: *"My task as Leader of the Lion is to lead the Lion through its transformations. I take the Lion down with me into the Underworld. At the Nadir of the Underworld, I will resurrect him and we will journey to the stars."*

Now Inanna starts to radiate and give off light. I see her become increasingly brighter and transform into an eight-pointed star, Venus! My heart beats quickly in anticipation. I long to become one with her. My heart swells and grows. Her light intensifies; She shines like a star in the night. The Goddess of Beauty shows her most seductive light to me. My heart merges with her heart. We become one essence. Inanna jumps on my back, takes my mane into her hands and thus she steers me. Together we ride at full speed. In the distance I see the Mountains of Sunset where the Sun is about to sink below the horizon. Inanna pats me on the breast and speaks encouragingly:

The Old Lion

"Come on Heru, let us follow the Sun. The journey of your transformations takes us into your Underworld. From this point on you will need to surrender your will to the Will of the Deep. When the cycle of the year grows towards its highest light, we reach the next stage of the Transformations of the Lion; at Whitsun the Old Lion achieves illuminated consciousness, as a result of the Great Work. About these mysteries I cannot speak to you now... After that the transformations continue."

The Sacrificed King

"The next stage of transformation is the Sacrifice of the King. It happens on the peak of the Summer Solstice. On this day the Solar King dies, and I drag the deceased king with me through the Gates of Death. The mysteries that I represent were practiced in ancient Sumer, Akkad and in ancient Egypt. These mysteries have been handed over mouth to ear, through generations of initiates of the highest order. At this point the path of personal growth ends and the Initiation Cycle begins. Here I use my sickle to cut the throat of the Solar King."

Now Inanna takes her sickle. She embraces me with all her love. I feel completely loved and accepted by the Goddess. She caresses and kisses me. She talks to me with sweet words: *"Let me see you, let me hear your voice. Your voice is sweet; your eyes are lovely.*

My lover, you belong to me and I to you. My love is as deep as death, relentless, with the flames of a blazing fire. Deep waters cannot quench love, nor floods sweep it away."

Then she lays me down and bites my throat. I feel warm fluid gushing over my chest. My life force is leaving me. I get dizzy, with every beat of my heart my blood gushes into the earth. My spirit becomes disconnected from my body, and I feel how I am dragged downwards. My blood is absorbed by the soil. I feel my spirit sink into the Inner Earth, downwards at full speed while Inanna is still merged with me. Her voice speaks to me from mind to mind. I also hear Idris's thoughts. All my other senses are gone. Inanna speaks to me from mind to mind in realizations and wisdom of pure and abstract ideas. I will try to translate into words what happens to me during that journey into the deepest layers of the Inner Earth:

§ 39. The Underworld Battle

"You have broken the First Seal, Heru. Stay with me and I will lead your disembodied spirit through the Seven Layers of the Deep. Like there are seven levels in Heaven, there are seven layers in the Deep. They mirror each other. Every level of the Deep needs to be explored. You will meet chaotic spirits that cause serious disruptions in your life, and in the lives of those under your jurisdiction. This is the place to set things straight. This is the place to get them under your conscious control. This is the place where the

Underworld Battle begins. Here you need to bring all the chaotic and opposing forces under your full control. The name of this place is the Dark Castle of King Herla."

I am dragged downwards, deeper and deeper into the Dark Castle. I meet many beings. They hide their true identities behind masks. Some disguise themselves as helpful forces, others are straightforwardly scary. They obstruct me and fight me. Inanna fights at my side to get them under her control. I hear Inanna's voice roaring when she battles the opposing forces. She roars like thunder:

"Away with you, piss off! Obey me, for I am the Lady of Battle, Goddess of all the fearsome creative powers. I am clad in terror, riding the great magical powers: The Great Mountain trembles when I ride to battle. I wield the mace, my arrows are prepared, my sling stones are ready for my rope, my lance is sharp, my axe takes down all evil-doers; for I am the Ruler of the Sacred Fire! I set fire to thick forests. I ride naked on the back of this lion, while I destroy the Wicked. Respect me, fear me, for I am Inanna, the Leader of the Lion, the Queen of Heaven, on my way to the East!"

From all corners new chaotic spirits approach me: I see all my weaknesses embodied, my character flaws personified, my suppressed fears surfacing. I hear the voice of Idris: *"Give your daimons names, Heru, and you will get power over them."*

Fighting we go downwards, together we penetrate the darkest places of the Deep. Inanna and I arrive at the deepest and most sinister area of the Dark Castle. Here, deep in the Inner Earth I meet Herla, and her... the dark twin sister of Inanna, the Queen of the Underworld... eye to eye I face her. She lifts her left arm and I see that she holds my lion fur coat in her hand. Inanna's dark twin sister takes my skin and takes a large nail and a hammer. Then with loud echoing bangs, she hammers my skin to the wall of the Underworld.

The Flesh of the Lion

The Dark Queen of the Underworld points at my fur: *"Behold, the Flesh of the Lion. I will preserve your costume, Heru. You have been sacrificed because your true nature as the Wounded King is that you are a vegetation spirit. Born in spring, you reign until summer. It is my job to ritually kill you at the harvest. Because of the deep Mysteries that are attached to these rites, I can only disclose the brief outlines of these secrets to you at this point."*

I feel completely and utterly helpless. My fur hangs on a nail in the deepest Cave of the Underworld. I am totally at the mercy of the Dark Queen. My blood has left my body; my senses are numbed. Is there anything I can do to save myself from this situation? Then an idea dawns on me. I think of my Batocchio and with the strength of my mind and with the help of my imagination and of all my inner senses I strongly visualize my magical wand and tap it three times.

The first time I tap it I hear the voice of the Dark Queen: "*I will keep you in the deepest Cave of the Underworld ... until the time comes when I will resurrect you to be reborn as the Soul of Light at Winter Solstice.*"

The Grip of the Lion's Paw

The second time I tap it, she continues: "*When that time has come, I will resurrect you through the Grip of the Lion's Claw.*"
And I feel the claw of the lioness touching me .... Where? I don't have a body ... but when I look around, I realize that I can see again. I see the Guardian of the Gates of the Underworld. She holds a great sword in her hands, with it she taps on my shoulder and then opens the stained-glass door of the Sun.

I tap on the floor for the third time, and I now feel how I completely merge with the Light. Then I hear the powerful voice of Eternity echoing and thundering all around me:

I ignite the Stars in your Eyes
Develop the Grace of your Illuminated Spirit
Nurture the Soul of Light that lives in your heart
Behold, the Inner Light burns bright,
It illuminates the Deep Oceans Inside
Behold: the Flammae Sacerdotal!

I feel the Light of my true essence burning and illuminating my heart, and a new body forms: a body completely built from Light. I connect with that body. I sense how my powers rise; I feel my strength returning. On top of that, I notice wings growing on my back. Surprised, I scan how they feel, I test my new muscles. I stretch my wings and sense the lifting pull of rising air. Will I be able to fly? I move my wings and feel how I am lifted upwards.

The Winged Lion

The Winds carry me and I fly higher and higher. When I flap my wings, I see the landscape becoming smaller and disappearing beneath me, I see the castle and the mountain far below me. I fly to the place where the air grows thin and stars start to twinkle in the sky. Here I am, powerful, courageous and free! I have faced all my inner daimons and overcome them. I am the one and only King of my Inner World. I have accomplished all my transformations and now have developed into the Winged Lion. As the King of my Inner Kingdom, I rule the Underworld, the Earth and the Heavens. From my high position I look over the landscape. I see Cadair Idris lying deep below, I look down on the Grail Castle on top of the mountain. I am no longer a prisoner of that Castle. I am now able to live in it and rise above it.

But I am still very curious about what happens inside the building. I realize that if I am free to rise above it, I am also free to explore the Castle further. I decide to land on the roof and enter again. I open the door. I descend down the stairs and find my way inwards, back into the Cave of Courage again. In the Cave of Courage, a female goddess waits for me. It is Inanna, the Leader of the Lion. In front of the door there stands a lantern. Idris points at the lantern and indicates that I pick it up: *"Heru, ignite the lantern with the Light of your Spirit. Speak the words Eternity taught you to illuminate your Inner Worlds with the Light of the Spirit."*

I ignite the Stars in my Eyes
I develop the Grace of my Illuminated Spirit
I nurture and protect the Soul of Light that lives in my heart
Behold, my Inner Light burns bright,
Illuminates the Oceans Inside:
Behold: the Flammae Sacerdotal!

I illuminate the candle by touching the wick with my Batocchio. The flame sparkles and dances on the wick. Then I open the door of the Leader of the Lion and step into the Hall of the Mountain King. I walk towards the Round Table and put the lantern on the surface. I look at the Wounded King in expectation, and he looks into my eyes and states: *"Behold the Flammae Sacerdotal. But that is not the only gift that the Inner Planes have given you. You also need to place the shard from the Mirror of Heaven on the Round Table."*
I reach into my pockets and take out the shard. Idris points out where I need to put it: on the segment of the Round Table - where the hieroglyph for the star sign of Leo is engraved

in gold into the lapis lazuli blue surface. As soon as I have put the shard onto the table, I become aware that it reflects the Tarot card of the Leader of the Lion, and it mirrors the stained-glass door in the wall. Then my attention is drawn to a flickering from an unknown source of lights on the table that I haven't seen thus far.

"Yes", Idris declares, *"come and walk with me around the Table."* Idris walks with big steps. He is a powerful figure, with his wand of power in his left hand and his swirling robes. *"At the star sign of Aries, you will also find a piece of the mirror. Look here, it depicts the door of the Wounded King. If you take a look at the image you see on the Tarot card you will find that his title is the Fisher King. The reason for that title will become clear in due time. On the star sign of Taurus, the shard reflects the Tarot card of the Hierophant. He gave you the Golden Bough. On the next star sign – Cancer – you will find the card for the Boat of Heaven. Here the Goddess Inanna helped you sow some of the Seeds that Eternity gave you before your Descent. Remember you established the Enchanted Lands and sowed the nut of the Tree of Life in your magical garden.*

Today you visited the constellation Leo and met Inanna, in her aspect of the Leader of the Lion. She helped you to find the Light of the Spirit, the Flammae Sacerdotal. This sacred flame is now burning in your heart, and every time you start a new inner journey, you consciously contact this Inner Flame by lighting a candle on your altar at the beginning of your meditation."

Then I see the obsidian mirror again. Next to it lies the papyrus scroll, sealed with seven seals. Seven?...When I look closer, one of the seals is broken. In front of the stained-glass door of Leo the two figures still sit on their carved thrones. Above them a banner with seven sigils flies. The woman sits motionless on her throne of ivory. She contemplates the murder of her enemies. The king stares directly at me. Suddenly he moves. He takes off his mask and reveals not a face, but the starry void... He rises and speaks the affirmation:

I ignite the Stars in your Eyes
I develop the Grace of your Illuminated Spirit
I nurture and protect the Soul of Light that lives in your heart
Behold, your Inner Light burns bright
Illuminates the Oceans Inside:
Behold: the Flammae Sacerdotal!

Then I see the fallen Tarot Card on the floor. I bend over to grab it. On it I clearly see the picture of the Leader of the Lion. I carefully tuck it away into the pouch that hangs on my belt, and find that the cards of the Fisher King, the High Priest, and the Boat of Heaven have also somehow manifested in my pocket.

§ 40. Exercise: The Creation of the Magical Paradise Garden

Idris smiles: "Yes, you have collected and internalized four shards that fell from the Star Mirror. But the work is not over yet. First of all, let us repeat the exercise of the Paradise Garden. Learn it by heart and perform this exercise every time you switch your consciousness from the profane world to the Enchanted Lands:

Step 1

Walk to the northern side of the hall, and see the landscape of the winter season painted on the northern wall of the Hall:

- In the North, you will find the country of Falias, it is as dark as the night. You look at a winter landscape where a blizzard dresses the scenery in a mantle of snow.

Then Idris walks around the table to face the East. Here the scenes of the spring season are painted on the wall as well:

- In the East, the Sun rises in the country of Gorias at a new dawn and the leaves of the plants and their flowers unfold in anticipation of a spring day.

I follow Idris as he walks further around the circumference of the table to face the South, and I study the painted scenes of the summer season:

- In the South, you oversee the country of Findias, a dusty summer landscape. Vine branches grow on the slopes. They stand in rows, their branches gently touching each other. They look like dancers holding hands, ready for a round dance. Further away, the slopes are planted with succulents and cacti. In the distance, you see a spewing volcano.

Idris proceeds to the West and I take the painting of Autumn into me:

- In the West, the Sun is setting. The sky slowly deepens its colors from azure into cobalt blue and the clouds change from white to yellow, orange and purple. In this spectacular display of color, the Moon rises above an endless ocean. Foaming waves rush ashore. The dune forests are adorned with yellow red foliage and show you that autumn rules here.

“The next times you visit the Inner Planes, do this exercise before your meditation while you walk around your altar with your Batocchio. Then you say this affirmation:

Step 2

I am the Power that grows
the Sacred Garden of the Soul
I clothe all the Forces of the Spirit
In a Garment of Thought and Speech
So that they manifest.

Step 3

The next step is to illuminate the candle on your altar while saying:

I ignite the Stars in my Eyes
I develop the Grace of my Illuminated Spirit
I nurture and protect the Soul of Light that lives in my heart
Behold, my Inner Light burns bright,
Illuminates the Oceans Inside:
Behold: the Flammae Sacerdotal!

Step 4

Then you sit down and relax thoroughly. When you have done that, the next step is to invoke the Hall of the Mountain King while reciting this spell:

Now do I descend into the Inner Seas
Whose Waters rise and fall within my soul
Now let the Inner Elements be seduced and still

Let me immerse myself into those Living Waters
And emerging therefrom
Let me bring from latent stress to potent image
The symbol of the King's High Table

I tap with my Batocchio and see how the double doors swing open, the nebula drift apart, and I step into the Great Hall with the black and white tiled floor and the stained-glass doors. The Wounded King is still moaning on his bed. Nothing has changed in regard to his situation. Many healers have been visiting him since the last time I visited him, but the deep wound in his groins is still bleeding. I greet him and assure him that I will do my utmost to find a solution. I tell him what I have discovered so far:

"Dear King, this time I am coming to share with you the miracle of the Transformations of the Lion and the appearance of the Flammae Sacerdotal on the Altar of the Spirit. I will illuminate this hall with its sacred light. I have brought my lantern and ignited the candle with the flame that burns deep inside of my heart. Maybe this flame will yield a permanent cure."

The Wounded King sighs: *"With each trial, I grow stronger in spirit, yet I wonder if this wound is meant to be my companion."*

Then Idris speaks again: *"But for now it is time for you to return to the profane world."* I tap three times with my wand on the floor. I feel how the mists enclose me again. I become aware of my physical surroundings. I feel my body, I stretch my muscles while I repeat the spell, I wake up in the physical world, feeling great.

IX ♍ WALKER BETWEEN THE WORLDS י

Trump IX – Virgo – ♍

The Walker between the Worlds

The Magus of the Voice of Power,
The Prophet of the Eternal

Hebrew letter	**Yod** י
Meaning	**Hand**
Simple Letter	**Sexual Love**
Path color	**Green - Yellowish**
Sign	**Virgo**
Path	**Tiphareth to Chesed**

Isolation and loneliness: divine reconciliation through isolation

Thirty-Two Paths of Wisdom:

The Twentieth Path is the Intelligence of Will, and is so called because it is the means of preparation of all and each created being, and by this intelligence the existence of the Primordial Wisdom becomes known.

§ 41. The Cave of the Walker Between the Worlds

I practice and work with the power of the sacred flame in my heart. I tend to the flame with all my love. I feel how I grow and how it gets easier to find the right solutions to problems in my life. Then I start to feel a growing desire to embark on my next journey to the Hall of the Mountain King, eager to hear how the Wounded King is doing since I last bestowed my magical gift upon him. Grasping my Batocchio tightly, I recall the spell Idris taught me. I focus on the image of the Double Doors in my mind, then tap the wand on the ground three times, whispering the incantation.

I am grabbed by the magical vortex and feel the now familiar transformation into the enchanted reality. On my arrival in the Hall of the Mountain King, I immediately walk towards the King to ask how he is doing. The King tells me that his situation is still the same, the wound still does not heal, it throbs, and it is inflamed. Then I ask him an honest question: *"My dear King, what else is happening to you? Does your wound have only disadvantages, no benefits? I would expect that you are growing in strength because of this ordeal. I see you do become stronger. Would you trade your pain for strength, if that were possible?"*

The King answers: "Yes, I do become stronger, but at what cost? My court is suffering because of me, too. If I used my pain to grow, would I then become blind to the suffering of those around me?"

This gives me something to think about, but I cannot contemplate on the King's dilemma for too long because Idris appears on the scene again. In his own magical way, he condensates in the Hall.

Idris speaks: *"As the Sun moves through the seasons, it illuminates the glass doors one by one. Last time you visited the hall it was the season of Leo. But now it is the end of the Summer. Let us witness how the Doors to Virgo open."*

I watch the Sun moving outside the hall and see how the stained-glass door of Virgo becomes illuminated. I see how a new part of the broad golden band forms, which connects the doors of Leo and Virgo. The representation on the stained glass becomes visible. It shows a Hermit carrying a lantern and holding a wand with a dragon on top. Idris gestures with his wand and says: *"Behold, let us consult the Walker Between the Worlds."* Then Idris indicates that I have to tap with my Batocchio. Immediately I feel all the physical sensations of the shift between the worlds. I am very curious about the nature of reality will be like in the next Cave I am allowed to visit.

I step through the stained-glass door. A deep relaxation takes me over as I feel the mists rising again around me. I become aware of that strange feeling, which I now recognize as the shift between the worlds. I am passing the Veil between the Worlds that takes me into other dimensions of time and space. where I will end up this time, and whom I am going to meet.

When the mists start to take shape, I slowly become aware of my environment. I notice that the path takes me into a large forest. I notice the small trails around me that tell me that these woods are inhabited by a lot of wildlife. Beneath the trees I see traces of badgers and fox dens. In the distance I hear the echoing hammer of a woodpecker.

Under my feet I feel twigs breaking and I become aware of walking into an open space in the woods. The sky is shifting in color. The golden rays of a late afternoon fade away and the light starts to shift to shades of blue. In the sky, the stars appear one by one: a token that the Star Goddess approaches the Earth. I recognize the appearance of Mercury and Venus. The Moon also surfaces from below the horizon and illuminates the trees with a silver light. This is the month of the star flowers. In the twilight I see the branches of a barren tree, crowded with twinkling stars, outlined in the silver moonlight. These stars resemble the stars in the sky; it is as if the starry night has descended and embraces the Earth.

"Do you recognize this land, Heru? Do you recognize your Tree?"
Shocked I look around me and I see that the Elemental Markers of my enchanted garden have grown into huge trilithon stones that reach the sky and create doorways into the Enchanted Lands? The nut I had been given by Inanna has grown into a full tree! The Circle of Stones surrounds its star crown.

Suddenly a figure approaches, he comes from the surrounding woods. A bearded man, he is hardly visible because of his camouflage. He wears a long dark green mantle with a hood that covers his head. In his hand he carries a strange looking object; it resembles a lamp, or is it ... a bird cage? In a wooden frame that hangs from his hand a sparkling fire dances. The shape of the flame reminds me of a fire bird, a phoenix. In his other hand he holds a staff of power. A large living dragon encircles its pole.

The man approaches me and nods his head in a gesture of greeting. He speaks in a low voice: *"Greetings Heru, how wonderful that you have received my invitation. The fact that you are here to meet me is a token that you are capable of answering to messages that are broadcasted on the Inner Planes. The reason I have asked you to come here, in the name and under the protection of the Mysteries, is that I want to take you to a special place in the Otherworld, called Merlin's Esplumoire."*

§ 42. Through the Gates of Wonder

Then the guide lifts his staff and explains: *"This is the famous staff that is capable of splitting the seas and creating a way through the Mists of Time."*
He knocks three times with the staff on the forest floor and in the twinkling of an eye I see the mists rise up again. The winds start to whirl around me and create a powerful vortex of leaves that rise up from the forest floor. I witness a deep stillness pervading the scene. I become aware of structures that materialize in the mists. Idris looks at me and instructs

me: *"Learn to watch with the Inner Eye and to hear with the Inner Ear, for there are many things that may happen in this place that are unknown to the outer world."*
I witness how the Star Tree starts to grow. It quickly encloses me and grows around me in the shape of an immense tower; no, not a tower, but a complete castle! While I watch, the branches that surround me color golden green and the Star blossoms start to open. I wonder what adventure I am entering...

§ 43. The Cave of the Walker

The Tree-castle doesn't stop growing. It climbs into the skies higher and higher, until the branches touch the body of the Star Goddess and caress her gently on the powerful winds. I look upwards to the enormous tree-castle: every flower merges with a star on the garment of the Star Goddess. The tree tower grows until it reaches the North Star. I watch the Heavenly Vault and I notice that it turns around one central point. Idris points upwards: *"High above us, you can clearly see the Polestar, Arcturus, that lovely Lamp of the North. It dances together with the stars of Ursa Minor, around it Ursa Major indicates the seasons of the year. Ursa Major, the Great Bear, is called Arthur's Wain by the Celts. Merlin's Enclosure is coming about around us, a cosmic spinning spiral of stars, turning around one point, as if turned by a giant hand."*

Then the guide points toward the circle of stones outside of the Castle: *"These great Trilithons are as old as time. They mark the secret patterns of the Universe, the North, the East, the South and the West. They are just like the stones that mark your Garden, but these mark the cardinal directions of the Universe. They are the high thrones for the cosmic Elemental Guardians: the Winged Human Being in the North, the Winged Bull in the East, the Winged Lion in the South and the Eagle in the West. In the central hall of the castle you will find a circular altar, made of dark lapis lazuli blue stone, ready to receive the regalia. Upon it shines the perpetual light of eternal spiritual reality."*

"Do you have ears to hear? Listen to the Silence and listen to my low clear call to all those who are worthy to serve my Mysteries. Do you wonder who I am? I am the Walker between the Worlds. Some know me as Merlin the Mage, but I have been called by many names in the cultures that have walked the Earth. While you are invited to explore this magical place where I am enclosed, become aware of your own motivation to visit me here: become conscious of the deepest aspirations of why you are here."

A white calm falls over me. There is nothing between that dim wilderness of thorns and flowers and the vast sweeping blackness filled with quivering stars. I look around to sense the nature of this strange place. This structure is both a Castle, a Star Tree and a Mountain. It is both an enclosure and a sacred place and a secret journey. I ask Merlin to reveal to me the secret path that is hidden in this place.

Merlin opens his arms and inhales the Winds of Wonder that still sweep around and cause this great atmosphere of Magical Power. Merlin utters the all-powerful Word, the Chord that connects the entire Universe. He resonates the most powerful spell of all spells:

"I call upon you, Nimue, join me. I call upon my Eternal Love!"

A new appearance forms in the Magical Mists, the beautiful shining figure of a lady clad in pure white robes. When she approaches, I notice that her skin is whiter than the foam of the Moon and her eyes are like a starlit dewy dusk.

While the lady materializes, I notice that Merlin moves to a position behind me. I feel his mind touching my spirit. He asks permission to share his true nature with me and to teach me about the nature of the eternal love that is between him and Nimue. When I give permission, Merlin steps into my Sphere of Sensation and begins to merge his consciousness with mine. My awareness starts to deepen and expand and grow into Cosmic Awareness. I realize that Merlin shares his sensations, his memories and his wisdom with me as if he and I become one. I feel how deep memories take me back into the past. A whirlwind of ancient memories rushes through me and I feel as if I live through those events.

§ 44. The Nature of the Cave

The memories start on that fresh spring morning eternities ago when Merlin and Nimue were courting. It is such a wonderful day, a day on which everything that takes place is full of meaning. A day on which the whole creation is dancing. The rhythm of everything that lives is reflected in the dance of all beings – be they creatures of a single spring day, or plants or trees or humans, the rocks and the rivers, the Earth itself or the Stars. I fall in love with Nimue; I truly desire her and admire her beauty which she is very willing to give. As I am longing for her intensely, she asks me a question:

"Oh Merlin, I admire the skills in the magical arts you have. I want to be your student and learn everything there is to know from you. Can I ask you to teach me how to make a beautiful place wherein I can work the Magical Arts?"

I answer that I will be happy to teach her. I show her how to create a very powerful circle in which true magic can take place. I show her how I invoke my Enchanted Lands. I take her as my student and show her wonderful magical places. I show Nimue a rock in which a great miracle is hidden. In order to unravel the magic of the mysterious rock I take her with me underneath that great stone. Nimue is so sweet and lovely that I am pleased to show her all the marvels there. My love for her increases. I look into her wonderful eyes, admiring her beauty and her intelligence and then she asks me the next question:

"I wonder whether it is possible to create a work of magic whereby I can lock up a man in such a way that no one can reach him nor that he can ever escape. A place where we could dwell together as long as we wish."
I answer*: "I can make you such a place".*
Nimue's voice becomes very soft and flattering: *"You are such a great mage; I want to be taught by the best. I don't want you to do it for me. No, I want you to teach me how I can do it by myself!"*

Then I start to explain to her exactly how to create such a place and Nimue takes notes and writes down every detail. I tell her that this particular type of magic belongs to a very fundamental part of nature:
"Nimue, you need to realize that all things are born, they live and die to be reborn again. This is woven into the web of life. In this way the soul of the Mage revolves as well and spirals through the cycles of nature. In order to renew myself I need to transform. In order to do so I merge with the Phoenix, that mysterious bird that burns its old form."

I lift my lantern, or is it a bird cage? I show Nimue the sparkling light: *"My true nature is Light. The Secret of the Castle in which you can lock up a man is encrypted in a bird cage. This bird cage contains a sacred road by which an old Earth walker can transform into a Soul of Light."*

I take a close look at the bird in the cage that I hold in my hands. It sparks off light, it is a real fire bird. Its plumage is partly red, partly golden. The size is almost exactly that of the eagle. The flaming bird is entirely covered with myrrh.
Then I look at Nimue and continue my teaching: *"The secrets of transformation are held within the Weaver's song; it is the dance of one who desires to become a Soul of Light. In order to achieve this transformation, one has to be free of the limitations of the profane world."*

Once the teaching is finished, we celebrate our love together. Nimue takes my essence into herself; she holds Eternity in her lap, like a white flower, or a star in the sky... I fall asleep and Nimue takes her long veil and with it she encircles the Star Tree and creates the enchantment I have taught her... Nine times she encircles the space and repeats the Magical words:

§ 45. Nimue's spell

Now for you I weave some weaving, so listen to it well
Now for you I twist some twining, become enchanted by my spell
Listen to how I weave the words while your eyes go blind
Listen with your heart while your soul becomes entwined

In the darkest night the silence breaks with the sound of an owl
The bushes start to rustle and the dogs begin to howl
Then you will pluck the stars of knowledge and you will become wise
And I will come to meet you, while your spirit flies

I will come to you, my love with the passing of the days
And I will set you free, each time your heart is bound in chains
From far beyond the Crystal Sea, I can hear your whispered dreams
And I will hear you're longing for the light of the Sun's Beams

Who are you?
You are a spark of light
A star in the night
A stone on the hill

But most of all: a fool out of time
But time is a circle without beginning or end
Wherein every event transforms and transcends
In the hub of the wheel you will find the hidden key,
It is called True Love, come and seek for me

And when your heart is light again and all your pain is gone
I will steal a Seed of Light; I will pluck it from the dawn
You will burn like a Phoenix and shed your skin
You will emerge as a Soul of Light at the new beginning.
Then you will fly through the lights of the starry way
From the darkness into the light of a newborn day

§ 46. Merlin's Birds nest

I now feel how the essence of Idris comes back onto the scene and I greet him. This time he appears in front of me. From the other side a white lady approaches me, Nimue! I am surprised as I listen to the words she speaks:

"By means of my magical powers I open things that have been closed, and close things that have been opened. One of my tasks is to rule over the celestial hinges at the back of the Northern Wind, around which the millstone of the world revolves. I have created an Otherworldly observatory for you. As the guardian of the borderlands between this world and the other, I can open the door between these worlds. In this way I can enable you to enter into all the secret Caves in any form you like, to shed your old form and renew yourself eternally in this Esplumoire of glass. Look around you: at this level of the

Hawthorn Tower, I have created 78 doors and windows. This place is the center of the Universe and from here you can receive glimpses into the future."

I look around and I see 78 stained glass windows. On every window glass I see the image of a tarot card. I realize that this is a place of great power, from here I can overlook the entire creation, enter into every reality, shapeshift into any form and prophecy!

Nimue continues: *"If you pay close attention to your surroundings and the wisdom teachings that you have been given, you will realize that every enclosure is an illusion. Through your thoughts, your will, your dreams, your desires, and your imagination, you can liberate yourself from any situation you are in. You can choose to free yourself of all the reactive patterns some folks call fate. Bondage only comes to pass because you are ignorant of these patterns. Heru, search your depths and seek yourself. Learn that you are nowhere to be found. Search the worlds from end to end and you will never find yourself or me. But call upon me, and I come at once. Need me, and I am by your side. Lose yourself and it is me whom you shall find."*

§ 47. The Affirmation for the Soul of Light

Then Merlin separates his essence from me, I feel a great loss when he disconnects. Then he speaks: *"Come and share in my meditation. I preside at my Mysteries, for I am the Hermit, the Magus and the High Priest. I call all mankind into union with me, and into my High Priesthood. Whoever will share my priesthood must share my contemplation. Humanity is the priesthood of the world and I am the Priest of the Universe."*

"See, I carry stars in my hand. Let yourself be guided by your star, your Flamma Sacerdotal, for the Light of Divinity is within you. Listen to the affirmation of the Soul of Light. Learn that beyond the darkness of your world there is light. You shall find yourself in me. You are because I am. Know me, and you will know yourself. Know yourself and you shall learn to know me better. I will be that which you shall become yourself. I will be that what you become as I am. Observe the Silence between the noises. If you have ears to hear you will hear the Voice of Merlin in between the Voices of Nature. I speak to all who are open to the Mysteries."

Then Nimue asks me to give her my pouch. She picks out the star which Eternity has given to me. When she holds it in her hand, I suddenly realize that it is the egg of a phoenix: *"In plucking a seed from the stars, you break through to a new awareness, and you will find the path to freedom. You come forth from my lap, Heru, for I have conceived you in the Hawthorn Tower."*

Merlin addresses me: "*Realize that you are the Soul of Light. Use the skills that you have been taught during this journey and ... gentle fool: find a new way of dancing! It will take you across the Abyss.* And I answer Merlin by the Affirmation of the Soul of Light:

I recognize you everywhere, in every scented flower,
I see you in the Eyes of the Night
I hear you in the voices of the day
I discover you in the arms of a child alone
I remember you in the mind of a stone.

I reach out my hand to take a gift from Nimue. As soon as I touch it, the lantern changes its shape and transforms into a bird cage.

While Nimue is weaving her magic, I become woven into the Hawthorn Castle, there is no possibility to escape. Soon the message of my disappearance starts to spread throughout the world. People start to speculate about my whereabouts. Some think this is caused by an enchantment of the faeries, others think I am busy with a great and preordained work of redemptive magic.

I hear the voice of Nimue. She answers: *"I will come to you as much as possible and then you will take me into your arms and we will make love.... and we will make love and we will make love ..."* An empty echo resonates through the castle.

Then I hear Idris' voice again. *"You need to realize, Heru, that the Castle is no prison, but a mystery to unravel. It is an enclosure of pure light. But for now, it is time for you to return to the Hall of the Mountain King."*

I sigh, taking in all that I have seen..... I tap with my wand on the floor and I watch the double doors swing open again. I see how the nebulae drift apart and I step into the Great Hall of the Mountain King, with the black and white tiled floor and the stained-glass doors. The Wounded King is still moaning on his bed. His situation is unchanged. All the healing that has been offered to him could not make his wound stop bleeding. I approach him and bow for him. I tell him what healing techniques I have learned on my journey with the Walker Between the Worlds:

"Dear King, this time I am coming to share the Mysteries of Virgo, the White Lady Nimue: I have learned that the Sacred Flame is a part of myself that I can carry with me wherever I go. I have been given a lantern, which is a bird cage at the same time. I have learned the Weaver's Song that teaches me how to unchain my heart from the material world and from the limitations of Time. In the hub of the Wheel of Time a mystery is hidden. In order to unravel this mystery, I need to listen to the Voice of Nature and solve the Mystery of the Star Seed. This time my gift to you is the Weaver's Song."

I sing for him and he greatly enjoys the beauty and the magic of this mysterious song. When I am finished the Wounded King answers: *"I am grateful for the remedy, yet I know this pain lingers — in some intangible way, it contains a lesson woven into my fate."*

Then it is time for me to go. I tap three times with my wand on the floor. I feel how the mists enclose me again. I become aware of my physical surroundings. I feel my body, I stretch my muscles while I repeat the spell, I wake up in the physical world, feeling great.

§ 48. Meditation

Meditate on the Weaving Spell and the Mysteries of Merlin's Esplumoire which Heru shares with the Wounded King. Make notes of your realizations.

*****

The Golden Ring in Summer

If you want to learn more about the myths belonging to the three tarot cards of the summer season, look at the website. In the shop you will find several video programs to deepen your knowledge even more:

https://www.hermeticartsandsciences.org/product/video-course-the-golden-ring-in-summer-tarot-journey-3/

Forthcoming are The Spellbinding Summer of Findias, and the Tapestries of the Goddess in Cancer, Leo and Virgo.

VIII ♎ The Hall of Justice ל

Trump VIII – Libra - ♎

The Hall of Justice

The Ruler of the Balance

Hebrew letter	**Lamed ל Meaning Ox Goad**
Simple Letter	**Work**
Path color	**Emerald Green**
Sign	**Libra ♎**

Thirty-Two Paths of Wisdom:

The Twenty-second Path is the Faithful Intelligence, and is so called because by its spiritual virtues are increased and all dwellers on earth are nearly under its shadow.

§ 49. The Cave of the Hall of Justice

I tap with my Batocchio and sit down in my meditation chair, and I project myself into the Hall of the Round Table. The images form quickly and in a detailed manner. Memories of the previous journeys cross my mind. The meeting with the Wounded King and the Inner Teacher, the Eros' lessons about love... I walk around the Round Table and I see all the images and stories I have learned reflected in the Shards of the Star Mirror. I notice that my previous journey into the Sacred Caves is already represented on the Round Table.

The King is still lying on his bed, covered in fur blankets. Today he is in a philosophical mood and shares his reflections on his illness: *"You know, Heru, this illness is not just a burden. It is also a teacher. The wound in my groin teaches me patience, and reminds me of my fragility and the vulnerability of life: it is a cruel tutor indeed!"*

I take a close look at the card of the Walker between the Worlds, walk back to the Leader of the Lion and recall the lessons about courage and the Transformations of the Lion. I look at the picture of the Boat of Heaven and recall the descent of the Goddess Inanna with her Sacred Me's. Then I feel the vortex, I see how the Door of Justice is lit by the Sun and opens, I hear a whisper...

"*Every living being will see my Boat of Light while it is sailing over the River of Gold. It encircles my Sacred Garden.*" .... The words resonate in my mind. Then I notice a sea mist rising: a thick impenetrable blanket of fog starts to envelop me. It obstructs my sight. I feel a strange dizziness. While I am being enshrouded by the mist, everything seems to turn around, shift inside out and upside down. I notice that Inanna steps out of my Body of Light, she leaves the boat and walks ashore while I remain seated. I watch her step on land and hear her words echoing in the far distance: *"I am Inanna and I bring down the Sacred Me's!"* ...

The connection is broken, the Goddess has left me and I am still sitting on the ship, feeling somewhat abandoned. Although ... on second thought ... is this the same ship? It is and it isn't. It is still a reed boat, but the style has changed completely. Instead of the canopy of stars, the baldachin over the throne is made of snakeskin. The Sea Horses at the prow have changed into a fire spitting Uraeus Snake. A shrieking hawk flies over the boat. To my amazement, I notice that the paddles of this boat are made from human bones and a human skull is fastened at the end of the paddles, they splash into the water. Everything I see has a typical Egyptian style. A strange figure pushes the boat off the shore: he is clad in a black and gold striped apron and wears a Jackal Mask that covers the upper half of his head and face. He turns his attention and speaks to me:

"Welcome on the next part of your journey, Heru. As you will realize, we are still travelling the Astral Seas. We are moving over a vast ocean that is covered with a thick layer of sea foam. Be careful what you think, be careful what you desire; every thought, every word, every emotion is a potential Thoughtform that will manifest immediately.

Our journey continues and you will become aware of the strange magic of the Otherworld outside of Time, that continuously influences the life of every being on your planet."

"In this part of the Astral Seas, this boat is named the Boat of Millions of Years. Look in the sky above you and watch the Constellations."
Anubis points at a group of stars: "O*n Earth they now live at that special time of the year, when the length of the day balances exactly with the length of the night. At the Autumn Equinox, the Forces of the Light will slowly start to give way to the Forces of the Night. From this day on, the Book of Heaven starts to open. It will become possible to read judgment on the deeds of every living soul. This will determine their future. This process begins while we sail into the Constellation Libra and pass the great Scales of Cosmic Balance."*

I clearly see two enormous scales in front of us, hovering between the stars around us. Two gigantic hands lift them. We sail through the Gate of the Scales and enter into a new region of the Universe. While the jackal headed figure steers the Boat of Millions of Years, he continues to explain what we see on our journey, while pointing at the stars around us and at those in the distance:

"Libra is the first part of what in antiquity used to be an enormous constellation: the Cosmic Scorpion Goddess Selquet. Her claws are the weighing scales of Libra, her body

is our modern constellation Scorpio, with the red beating heart of the star Antares as a marker point in the night sky. The third part of this ancient constellation is nowadays called Sagittarius, the Arrow of the Archer. In classical times it was the Sting of Death of the scorpion goddess Selquet. Libra's weighing scales become visible in the two stars Zuben El Genubi and Zuben El Chamali, the Southern and Northern Claw of the scorpion. Zuben El Genubi will teach you to always measure up your deeds to the highest ideals. Zuben El Chamali measures our deeds against leadership qualities. If you work with these stars they will arouse above all things spiritual and mental forces. But we have to pay attention elsewhere because you are being called by the Gods!"

§ 50. The Encounter with Ma'at

Suddenly the light changes. It is so bright that it becomes difficult for me to see anything. This light does not cast any shadow. It illuminates every corner of my being and I must admit that it is an extremely confrontational experience! Amidst this brightness a winged goddess becomes visible, she wears an ostrich feather on her head. Her eyes are like bright lights that penetrate deeply into my heart. With a dramatic gesture, she lifts the magical necklace that she wears around her neck, to the level of her mouth. She breathes over it while she whispers; *"I call up your heart!"*

And immediately my heart jumps out of my breast and hovers in front of me in empty space. Ma'at carefully takes my heart between her hands and looks into my eyes.

"It is time to clean 'the house.' It is time to cleanse your emotions. Sort out what is no longer useful or helpful to you, so that you can let it go. With the emotional balance you create in this way, you will open up new possibilities. Use this emotional space to get access to your spiritual knowledge and integrate it into your everyday life. However, make sure that, before you apply this wisdom, you really understand this knowledge!"

Then the Goddess carefully places my heart into one of her scales. She plucks the ostrich feather from her head and puts it into the other weighing scale.

Anubis explains: *"If your heart weighs the same or less than the feather, you will be able to continue your journey. But if your heart is too heavy and weighs more than the feather, the road will be blocked for you!"*

Ma'at continues: *"I am the personification of the Laws of Nature on which the world is based. Not just the physical laws, but also the Laws of Fate. I do not judge or condemn; I only keep the balance of the forces of nature. I correct everything that is not in harmony. Every person has instincts and talents for self-preservation and development towards goodness. If they are not correctly stabilized, they lead to distortion and destruction. I invite you to use our meeting as a precious encounter, an opportunity to Heal your Self. When you sail inwards into my realms, you will enter into the Hall of Truth. This will enable you to look straight into the Womb of the Great Mother; stare deep into the Inner Earth, like an ostrich. Calibrate yourself with that Truth beyond Time in the World of the Duat, the Realm of the Subconscious and Unconscious mind, and heal your emotional pain."*

§ 51. Into the World of the Duat

Anubis explains further: *"Heru, it is important for you to realize that in ancient times, the word 'death' did not only mean deceased. It was used for a variety of states of consciousness that give access to the Inner World. The ancient Egyptian ceremony of the Judgment of the Heart is not only for deceased people, it is also a healing ceremony for the living who seek to correct a disbalance. It can be a life-changing experience! By the Ceremony of the Weighing of the Heart you set Ma'at, 'order', in place of Isfet, 'chaos'." "*

"Look, the boat now enters into the World of the Duat. We will sail the Underworld River named Urness. We will dock at the Island of Fire, where we will visit the Cave of Justice, correctly named: the Hall of the Double Ma'ati. This is a Cave that represents a double truth, because there is not only the truth of oneself, but also the truth of the other. If you want to realize majestic greatness in your own life, you will need to set your Enchanted Lands in order!"

§ 52. The Judgment of Heru

In the harbor of Libra at the Island of Fire we are awaited by a large company of Gods and Goddesses. Anubis indicates that we should join the company. In a procession we walk into the direction of an Egyptian Temple. Before the entrance we have to wait, while we watch the Egyptian Gods entering in procession and taking their seats in the Hall of Justice. Then I walk through the aisle, flanked by two of the goddesses. I am invited to sit down on the throne on a dais, in front of the main altar. Then the two goddesses - Isis and The Leader of the Lion - wrap me in bandages of light. While I am sitting there, I think that I now must resemble a mummy. On my face they put the Death Mask of Osiris.
When I am completely wrapped up like a caterpillar, I look straight in the face of Ma'at, who stands directly opposite of me with outstretched wings. Her penetrating eyes look deep into my soul. I feel a cry welling up from the essence of my being:

"My Heart, my Mother,
My heart that I got from my Mother
Do not speak against me
when I stand before the Guardian of the Scales"

Then a choir of voices starts an incantation, all the Gods join in this enchantment:

Sleep, Heru, sleep the primordial sleep,
Ruler of your Inner Worlds, visitor of the Deep.
"Enter into the Duat wherein Truth begins to seep,
Answer to the Scales, Heru, and hear the Goddess weep!

I feel that I fall asleep and I am drawn into that Inner Reality where Words become experiences and my heart immediately responds.

Ma'at rises and speaks: *"Hail to thee, thou who seeks to achieve Majesty over the Inner Worlds, blessed is the Son of Eternity. I welcome you in the Halls of Judgment, here thy heart will be weighed."*
Then Ma'at looks to the assembled company of Gods and asks:
"Who shall speak for Heru with an honest tongue? And who shall speak against him?"
Two Gods with animal masks rise, they bow together and speak in turn:
"I, Anubis, son of Osiris and The Leader of the Lion will speak for Heru."
"I, King Herla, son of King Herla, will represent the opposition. I will speak against Heru."

The Leader of the Lion, who is standing behind me, starts an incantation. It sets a shiver down my spine:

"I call upon you, Winds of the West:
Hold Heru safe.
The Soul of Light sleeps the Healing Sleep.
Heru, follow the Setting Sun,
While you travel the Astral Seas
where every dream, every desire, every emotion manifests.
Sweet be the dreams of Heru!"

Isis joins the incantation and her beautiful voice lifts the atmosphere:

"I call upon you, Winds of the West.
Carry Heru to the Hall of the Double Truth.
Sweet Heru, Soul of Light,
my songs will lift your spirit and my heart goes with thee
while you traverse the darkness."

Then she spreads her arms and speaks with a firm voice: *"I weave a dream for my child, that it may safely travel through the Halls of the Double Truth. I weave a garment for*

Heru from the rays of light at the Golden Hour. Amethyst and gold are the garment in which Heru will enter into the Land of the Setting Sun. The sun's last rays will touch your forehead and this light will condense into a golden snake that protects it."

The Leader of the Lion repeats Isis' gesture and states: "*I take the stars at the Blue Hour and weave a cloak of indigo and Sirius shall be its clasp. From the moon's light upon the clouds I will make your sandals, the Vulture Goddess will descend and create a Crown for your head."*

Then both goddesses raise their voices and call upon the Forces of the Opposer: "*We call upon the assembly of Gods and Goddesses of Heaven, mighty is your judgment. We call you forth from the Deep, come and hear the voice of King Herla, feel the fiery rage of King Herla, the might and heat of the desert, the Opposer of the Soul of Light and the enemy of Heru".*

Then I hear the voice of Ma'at. She speaks directly to my heart: "*Here in my Hall of the Double Maati, the Truth is brought to Light. Realize that Truth always has two sides; your side and the side of the opposer. Based on this Double Maat the Gods will judge and the heart of Heru will be weighed and balanced."*

Anubis rises and speaks: "*It is time to open the mouth of Heru, so that the Soul of Light can answer the questions of the forty-two judges."*

Anubis takes three Magical Instruments that are hidden in between the stars: *"I take the Tools of the Midwife from the Starry Heavens to help you be born in the Otherworld. With the Magical Equipment of the Midwife, you are born into another dimension of your life. With the Adze I touch your mouth: Heru, open your mouth, I free your tongue and your throat so that your voice can be heard in the Hall of Justice!"*

Ma'at speaks again: *"I call upon the Gods to witness that I shall judge without favor between Heru and King Herla, for I am the servant of Truth. I set aside all blood ties and all the thoughts of my heart and judge according to the Law. It is time to call upon the forty-two Assessors to raise the right questions to judge the Heart of Heru. Heru, I want you to answer to all those questions in truth. Speak, o ye Gods! Speak, you mighty Hekau of the Two Lands and make yourselves known to the Lords of Justice."*

Now Ma'at kneels in the center of the hall and positions her scales. Her arms form the balance. Then she states: *"I am Ma'at. I am Truth and Order. I am born from Chaos and I put everything in its place. I am the Balance and I decide upon the Fate of Heru. I am Cosmic Balance itself."*

Anubis says: *"Bright Heru, you must undergo your judgement. In doing so you will show humanity that the Gods are also subject to Law and Order. Heru, are you ready for the prosecutors?"*

And you feel a cry of the heart welling up from the deepest parts of your soul: "*Oh, you Lords of the Halls of Justice, listen, for I offer myself up unto you and your judgement. Silence me not, for I speak with my heart. I come before you to answer for the choices I have made so far in my life on earth. Let the Sacred Way be opened before me, that I may follow the Sun and the Gods, let me pass through the Gates of the Light. The Gods live in me, as in every human being on earth. Speak to me! I rule my Inner Worlds; I will answer your questions.*"

Now the double doors of the hall swing open and forty-two judges enter in procession and take their places on the empty seats. When everyone is seated a great gong resonates through the hall and at a sign of Ma'at the judges rise one by one and put forward their question.

... This is the point where you evaluate your life and actual issues that are taking place, and ask yourself critical questions about your choices ...

I watch how my heart gently descends on the scales. Ma'at comes and lays her hands over them as before and I hold my breath... They balance exactly! While holding her hands over the scales, she looks into my eyes. Then I hear her voice: "*Heru is in perfect balance. Rejoice, for you will become the bright Soul of Light!*"

Anubis rises and states: *"Hail Heru, you rule your Inner Kingdom. This day is blessed, for you have opened the door between the worlds and have access to the light beyond."* All the Gods and Goddesses that are present in the Hall rise and start to clap: *"Heru, you are the Child of the Earth and the Heavens, you are Ruler over your Inner Kingdom, Hail!"*

Ma'at states: *"Remember always that Love has saved you, as love can save all humanity. Anubis, restore the heart of Heru and crown the Soul of Light as the ruler over his Inner Kingdom. Place the Double Crown upon Her's head and place the crook and flail in his hands. Release Heru from their bindings so that this Soul of Light may take its place among the Great Ones."*

Then Anubis walks to the scales and carefully he takes my heart into his hands, and places it carefully back into my breast. Isis and the Leader of the Lion release the bindings, and they place the crook and flail into my hands.

The Gods and Goddesses rise again and shout as a choir: *"Bright is the day that shall come, for Heru rules the Inner World! Let humanity rejoice, for Balance and Justice have just entered the world!"*

Then I hear Idris's voice again. *"You need to realize, Heru, that the Underworld is your own subconscious mind. Every personal wound, every deed that you wanted to forget, every injustice against you or that has been caused by you is part of the great River Urness, that carries the Boat of Millions of Years. But never forget that this is a river of pure light. But for now, it is time for you to return to the Hall of the Mountain King."*

..... On Idris's request I tap my wand on the floor and I watch the double doors swing open again, I see how the nebula drift apart and I step into the Great Hall of the Mountain King. The Wounded King is still moaning on his bed. He has a questioning expression on his face. I can see that the wound is still bleeding. I approach him and bow for him. I tell him what healing techniques I have learned from my journey to the Cave of Justice:

"Dear King, this time I participated in a ritual in the Hall of Justice. I was shown my own life and was held responsible for all my wounds and the wounds I have caused. I met King Herla and he was also given the opportunity to explain why he has caused such pain, because the Hall of Justice is the hall of the Double Truth. By placing myself in the shoes of King Herla I have learned that he is my shadow. If I bring my shadow to the Light, it will transform and I will heal. This wisdom is the gift I bring you this time."
The King answers: *"I will contemplate this wisdom, thank you, Heru."*

§ 53. Affirmation

Idris steps forward and provides instructions to use the Hall of Justice as a powerful healing tool, in case any injustice has been caused.

"The goal of this exercise is to restore balance in the heart, to gain understanding of the position of your opposer in a conflict, to get rid of any bad blood or feelings of injury. In this way a solution will be sought for that is in the best interest of all involved.

- Create a small altar with a symbol for Justice on it, for example a pair of weighing scales.

- Put two small candles on both sides of the scales.

- Put one chair in front and two chairs at both sides of the altar. Dedicate one seat to yourself – Heru - and the other seat at the opposite side of the scales to your opposer – King Herla. The seat in front of the altar is dedicated to the Goddess of Justice, Ma'at.

- Sit down on the seat of Heru, choose an issue from your life where you are being treated unjustly and write it down.

- Get up and put down your notes in front of the scales.

- Take the Feather of Truth from your pouch, place it on top of the note, and then you say the spell:

My Heart, my Mother,
My heart that I got from my Mother
Do not speak against me
when I stand before the Guardian of the Scales

- Take the seat that is connected to your own position in the conflict – the Seat of Heru. Withdraw into yourself and contemplate your side of the issue.

- Rise, thank the Goddess Ma'at for her attention and take the seat of Ma'at. Here you make notes of your realizations.

- Now you switch chairs and try to look at it from the opposite side – the Seat of King Herla. Place yourself in the shoes of the opposer and gather new realizations and insights into the situation from this perspective.

- When you are ready, make notes of the realizations of King Herla.

- Sit down on the Seat of Ma'at and see if the scales balance. Feel if your heart is open or not. If your heart is not open, warm and satisfied, the work is not finished.

- When you are finished with the issue, the scales will balance and your heart will feel free.

- When you are ready, you burn the paper and thank the Goddess of the Scales.

Now Idris taps on my shoulder as a sign that it is time to go back to the profane world. I tap three times with my wand on the floor. I feel how the mists enclose me again. I become aware of my physical surroundings. I feel my body, stretch my muscles while I repeat the spell, I wake up in the physical world, feeling great.

XIII ♏ THE TRUTH ABOUT DEATH נ

Trump XIII – Scorpio ♏

The Truth about Death

Child of the Great Transformers

Hebrew letter	**Nun** נ
Meaning	**Fish**
Simple letter	**Movement**
Path color	**Green – Blue**
Sign	**Scorpio** ♏

Thirty-Two Paths of Wisdom:

The Twenty-fourth Path is the Imaginative Intelligence, and it is so called because it gives a likeness to all the similitudes which are created in like manner similar to its harmonious elegancies.

§ 54. The Cave of the Truth about Death

א מ ת Emet - Truth

I tap with my Batocchio and sit down in my meditation chair, and I project myself into the Hall of the Round Table as usual. Having arrived there, I walk respectfully to the Wounded King and I ask him about his condition. He assures me that he benefits from my contributions to his healing, but unfortunately, they haven't cured his wound.
I ask the King: "*Do you still have hope? Do you believe in the possibility of healing?*"
The King replies: *"Hope is my only ally, yet every dawn I fight a battle against Herla's shadows that dwell within me."*

Then I walk around the Round Table and notice that the shard with the image of the Hall of Justice has been added on the Round Table. As usual, Idris appears in the Hall in his own unique way. It never ceases to amaze me when the nebula appears, condensing into a thick mist and the hooded figure steps out of the fog. Idris greets me and tells me that we have to make haste, because soon the Sun will rise in the constellation of Scorpio. Idris circumambulates the Round Table and checks whether all the shards of the Mirror of Heaven are on their place. Also, the band of gold grows after every constellation that has been visited. Now the band of gold starts in Aries and reaches the door to Scorpio.
After Idris has checked the Round Table, he walks towards the Door of Scorpio. He turns his head towards me: "*Do you want to experience Truth, Heru?*"

Then he speaks: "*We enter the Portal of Death, which is closely connected to Truth. In the ancient world the world, Death did not have the same meaning as in our culture. The ancient sages assumed that when you are born in the profane World, you die in the Otherworld. When you die in this world, you are born in the Afterlife. On top of that, they defined Death as a state of consciousness. In their opinion, the conscious state of Death has seven layers: there are Seven Stages of Death. The Portal of Scorpio will lead you through these seven stages, and you will learn the Truth about Death.*"

While the Sun starts to illuminate the portal, Idris raises his wand and starts to draw symbols on my forehead. He draws them from right to left: *"Aleph, Mem, Tau:* ת מ א*, Emet is the Hebrew word for Truth!*" Then I feel the vortex, I see how the Door of Death opens, I hear a whisper...

"Use your imagination, Heru, and change your arms into wings. Feel them and feel the joy and the freedom they bring. Feel the winds under your wings lift you up!"
I notice a strange transformation taking place. From my skin, feathers start to grow on my entire body and they itch! When I move my arms, I feel how they catch the air and I am already almost carried away by the wind. The transformation stops at my head, my head remains the same, I have changed into a falcon bird with a human head.

"*During this time of the year, you will shapeshift and travel as a bird, Heru, a Soul Bird. A Soul Bird is a bird with a human head. Spread out your wings and jump upwards!*"

I feel that the wind lifts me. Wow! This is sensational… I flap my wings and I see that the ground disappears further and further into the depths. I feel how the wind under my wings is carrying me. I climb higher and higher and I feel the joy and the freedom; I see the altitude perspective of everything that is around me. This is incredible… I feel totally alive from my feet to my wings; I float on the wind and feel it in my face.
I climb higher and higher and I approach the clouds. Then I enter into the clouds and I am surrounded by fine mist. I am unable to see anything else but grey floating nebula that surrounds me. I climb even higher and suddenly I am above the clouds and I see the sun radiating in front of me, the clouds floating below me, they take away my view on the landscape. They are white and reflect the sunlight from a distance. Then I see an enormous grey bird flying into my direction. It comes towards me and flies in slow circles around me. This is Nekhebeth, the Vulture Goddess. I see everything from a bird's eye view and I can hear what the great vulture is thinking. Nekhebeth circles around me slowly and then she invites me to fly with her.

She flies in the direction of the top of Caer Idris. I follow her and together we encircle the mountaintop. Nekhebeth carries an unidentified piece of meat in her beak. While I am pondering what this is, I hear a clear voice in my head answering:

"I carry your physical body in my beak, Heru. It is time to reveal to you the Truth about Death, because I, the Vulture Mother, am the Keeper of the Secrets of the Seven Stages of Death.

On your forehead there is written Truth: **ת מ א.** *When I remove the letter Aleph* **א** *– symbolizing the Breath of Life - from the word Truth on your forehead, it changes into the word* **ת מ:** *Met, meaning Death."*

Nekhebeth stretches out one wing and wipes the Aleph from my forehead. Then she releases my body from her beak. I see how my body tumbles down forever and smashes into bloody pieces on the top of Mount Caer Idris. To my amazement, I see myself from the altitude perspective as a deceased body, my corpse shattered into pieces on the ground.

I fly around in circles around the top of the Mountain of Salvation, I don't know what to do. The clouds move away and, somewhere in the depths, I see a small village, typical for the countryside. In the distance, I hear the ringing of church bells. I am drawn to the sound, curious about what is going on there. I am drawn in the direction of the sound towards my desire. I fly into a small chapel. I see that a coffin is just being carried into the church. The top of the coffin is covered by sweet smelling roses. A man clad in a hooded robe approaches the coffin. In his hands he carries seven roses that are still budding, he lays them on top of the coffin. I notice a ribbon with a name written on it. To my amazement I read my own name. I ask the hooded figure what the significance of this scene is, and he tells me that I will experience the first of the Seven Deaths.

He gives me one of the roses. The petals unfold as I hold the rose in my beak. I inhale the sweet smell. When I do this, the smell of the rose creates a whirlwind that takes me upwards in slow spirals. I am carried by the soft wind of sacred air. I am drawn up by a vortex. When I am high in the sky, I pass the clouds and I become aware that I am travelling back in time. I look down to earth.

I see how large clouds of hot gases swirl around and slowly coagulate. I witness how the enormous heat gradually starts to cool down, formatting a large volcanic surface. And I see the first places of solid rock, moist steaming gases rising from the surface of the Earth, geysers spraying hot water on the volcanic surface. I see the first land and witness how the waters gather together and form oceans. The creation of the first animal life, microbes forming in hot oceans, ever changing and growing. Plants develop on the shores of the primordial oceans and I witness the first animals crawl onto land, the surface of the Earth slowly becomes covered in large trees, creating a vast jungle where reptiles come to life. Again, I hear the Voice in my head: *"Everything has to change in order to grow, death is necessary to make place for new species. These animals were stepping stones for newer forms of animal life, and for the human life we know today. They had to die to make place for the new phase in the evolution of the planet."*

§ 55. The Vulture Mother

Now I hear her voice again, the voice of Nekhebeth, the Vulture Mother. I see her flying in slow circles over my dead body. *"This creature has passed away. I will take it into myself. I will pick all the tissue of this carcass, and I will take it with me to the high realms, because I am the Goddess of the Highest Heaven... I am the bird mother. I eat all your flesh, Heru, and take it into myself, until I have freed your naked bones, the bleak white bones that form the essence of your being. I take your bare white bones with me to the Above. My name is Nekhebeth, I am Mut, the Mother Goddess, I am the bird mother. I am a very old goddess. I take care of the souls after their death, and I take care that they are born into the Afterlife on the Inner Planes. Come with me, Heru, and visit the area above the clouds."*

I follow the bird mother. We fly even higher, and I notice that night is falling. The entire sky is covered with beautiful twinkling stars. In the starry heavens, the constellation Scorpio illuminates the sky. Nekhebeth flies even higher, and we approach the great Gates of Death.

Nekhebeth flies straight into a black hole that is surrounded by red rose petals. *"We have arrived at the Gate of the Great Transformer. Here is the Gateway between Life and Death"*. Nekhebeth flies above the spiral highway in space, and I follow her, heading for the Source, with my flesh in her stomach and my bare bones in her beak. As Nekhebeth flies into the black hole, my bones fall apart, the bone marrow is released. When that happens Nekhebeth descends, she takes the bones into her claws, and picks the bone marrow from my bare bones. Then I see how an egg forms in her body. I watch in amazement. I witness the miracle happening before my own eyes. I take a good look at the egg, and I look at the essence of my soul! I clearly see the Spark of Light, of my Life! I look at it against the light, and then I see the holographic image of my ever-changing soul, a myriad of aspects of my soul. I know that I have been in manifestation many times. All my memories of this soul are saved in this crystal egg.

§ 56. The Egg

Suddenly, the egg cracks and from the inside strange thoughtforms emerge. They float around the shards. They are all different forms of personalities that have carried my soul through my previous lives. They jump out from the essence and are projected outwards. I see thoughtforms of my former lives.

My soul egg turns, meditating on its own essence, projecting its experiences outside. All my previous experiences float around the egg, and dance around the core. They mirror themselves in that one essence.

Nekhebeth touches my mind again, and I clearly hear her voice: "*When the egg has meditated long enough on itself, the journey downwards starts again.*"
I witness how the Beautiful Road opens, the River of Stars that will carry my soul back through the Veils of Time. Nekhebeth says it is time for her to say goodbye and be on her road, as her task is to bring more souls to the source.

"Heru, you must now decide your destiny. This decision is based on your desires. The lessons you choose based on your desires will form the pattern for your next life. Choose which Classroom Caves will dominate it. Once the desire to learn new lessons grows in intensity and the right Caves have been chosen, a new descent will take place, and a new Path of Passion will open with new opportunities. I have brought you to the place where Eternity sits with her weaving loom, at the place where she weaves the Veil that divides the Worlds of the deceased and the living."

I watch how Nekhebeth flies away, downwards. I look around, and then I see Eternity, sitting behind her loom, she is weaving... She takes drops from the primordial ocean, and with this moisture she weaves bodies. She takes primordial moisture to form hair, nails, flesh and bones and everything she weaves, she puts into the egg. She carefully transfers the essence of my desires into my soul flame. Then Eternity opens the Beautiful Road for a new descent. Eternity prepares beauty. Sparks of light and sparks of nothingness are woven together into one being. Carefully the Zodiac is set in place to prepare the right circumstances for my new birth. The Beautiful Road takes me and downloads me into my new and improved body.

Suddenly, I feel a strong pull. I cannot resist the force, and I find myself being drawn into the womb of the Goddess. I am a fetus, and I drift in the primordial ocean within the womb of my mother. There I create my new body. The Goddess helps me weave my body by nurturing me, and the forces of fate provide the right circumstances for my coming life.

Thus, I create my new self. When this work is finished, I am born. I am born on an island outside of time.

I have traveled a long way to unravel these secrets, I have flown into the Heavens, seen the earth below. I have visited the highest heaven above the clouds, and passed through the Gate between life and death. Then I feel a pulsating pressure on my new body. I am pushed downwards from all sides. Where am I? Is this the Gate of Birth? Is this a new descent? I pass through this gate and ...

... on the other, side Idris is waiting for me at the stained-glass door of Scorpio. He greets me and draws the symbol of the Aleph א back on my forehead. I feel my lungs unfolding, filling up with the Breath of Life.

"Welcome Heru, you made quite a spectacular journey. You have learned the first Truth about Death. Now that you are reborn in the profane world, you have died in Heaven. This journey will have a real effect on your life, depending on what Caves you chose to fulfill your desire. Things will change for the better! Now I am very curious - what gift you will bring to the Wounded King?"

I sigh and turn inwards. What gift can I give the king? I approach his sickbed and sit down next to him. I take his hand and tell him that physical death is not the end. *"When you die, you are born in Heaven. Life does not end. In Heaven, you have the opportunity to choose a new fate for your next life."*

"That is all very good and true", Idris remarks. But you 'died' and were 'reborn' as well, Heru, while still alive! This is a gift for all true Mages and people who develop an inner world and are able to concentrate long enough to work in this alternate reality. The first Truth about Death is that you can visit the Inner Planes when you are able to go deep enough in meditation. There you can edit your life and apply changes which will manifest in your profane life. In this way you can heal old wounds, add new ideas and energies to your life: You become King over your own life!

"But for now, it is time to return to the profane world, Heru. It is time to reconnect with your physical body..."
Then I see my physical body sitting in my meditation room. I fly towards it and open the Door to my Heart, I enter into ... a bird cage, or is it a lantern? It is a place where my Inner Light lives, my Soul Bird lives, it is a gateway to the secrets of the Cosmos. I can go to this place every time I need to contact, or to feed my Inner Light. This is the light that I contact when I ignite the flame of my lantern on my altar. Now I merge with my physical body. I stretch my muscles, move my neck, and breathe consciously in and out. I become aware of my body again and I return to the Here-and-Now, feeling great and refreshed.

XIV GUARDIAN OF THE RAINBOW

Trump XIV - Sagittarius ♐

The Guardian of the Rainbow

Temperance - The Bringer Forth of Life

Hebrew letter	**Samech ס**
Meaning	**Prop**
Simple letter	**Anger**
Path color	**Blue**
Sign	**Sagittarius ♐**

Thirty-Two Paths of Wisdom:

The Twenty-fifth Path is the Intelligence of Probation, or is Tentative, and is so called because it is the primary temptation, by which the Creator tried all righteous persons.

§ 57. The Cave of the Guardian of the Rainbow

I tap with my Batocchio and sit down in my meditation chair, and I project myself into the Hall of the Round Table. As usual - the Wounded King lies on his bed, dressed with fur blankets. I look him in the eyes, and in my mind, the question forms whether his wound has improved. He responds to my asking face by shaking his head. *"The pain in my groins does not only handicap me - it isolates me and makes me lonely. Loneliness results in the silence in my Halls. The Enchanted Castle feels empty, echoing with my pain."*

With a sigh I release the air from my lungs. *"I will keep trying to find a cure for you, my dear king. That is why I am here. I am eager to learn what kind of healing is hidden behind the next stained-glass door".*

As usual I walk around the Round Table. I look in the direction of the next door, wondering what adventure lies behind this stained glass? Then the mist forms in the center of the hall. Idris greets me and tells me that I will visit the constellation Sagittarius. He checks the shards of the Mirror of Heaven; the image of the Seven Stages of Death has been added on the table. Also, the band of gold has grown, it starts in Aries and has reached the door of Sagittarius. Weapons are waiting for me beside the entrance of the cave, a beautiful rainbow-colored bow and a bag filled with arrows to carry over my shoulder. I hang the arrow bag and the bow around my chest.

We both walk towards the stained-glass door. Idris turns his head towards me and remarks; *"This time we are going back in time, Heru!"*

I stand before the Cave that is called the Guardian of the Rainbow. As usual I see the Sun rising behind the Stained-Glass window. When the sunrays hit the glass, I witness how a beautiful rainbow of colored light falls into the Hall of the Mountain King. Standing before the stained-glass door - I study its image - apart from the rainbow, I see a pair of hands holding a globe, and a naked man who is chained to that globe. He is wounded in his side. From the heaven comes an eagle flying down, which brutally tears off pieces from his liver. I hear the moaning of the man, trying in vain to suppress his pain. At the bottom of the image, a strange creature is depicted - it is half man, half horse. I see him shooting a burning arrow at the eagle. In the background, in the sky the outlines of a few constellations appear in the evening sky...

Idris raises his Dragon wand - and to my amazement - the dragon comes alive and exhales a fiery breath towards the door - which opens. Idris precedes me and together we walk downwards over an unpaved path. *"We are going back in time, Heru. Look around you - in these meadows live real mythical creatures."*

At both sides of the path, I watch strange and wild nature spirits playing in the meadows. I wonder what kind of creatures are they? They walk upright and have goat legs or horse legs? They have mane-like hair, bestial faces, and snub noses.

Idris sees my amazed face and points with his wand to the creatures; "*In these meadows - Muses play and Satyrs dance. Satyrs are extraordinary creatures. They are ecstatic: they love wine, music, dancing, and sex. They live in remote places, such as woodlands, mountains, and pastures. A special type of Satyr is the Centaurs. Centaurs are half human and half horse. They are wild creatures - heavy drinkers! They are regarded to be unreliable, misleading, crude, wild, and even adulterous.*"

"*However, there is one Centaur that is special. His name is Chiron. Chiron isn't like the others. He is the son of the Water nymph Philyra and Cronos, the God of Time. Chiron was conceived at a mythical island when the god Cronos, cheated on his wife with Philyra. But this act of adultery did not remain unnoticed: Cronos and Philyra were caught in the act by Cronos' wife. To escape her anger Cronos shapeshifted into a horse - leapt out of the bed and galloped off in the form of a long-maned stallion. Philyra stayed behind, feeling terribly ashamed. A few weeks later she discovered that she was pregnant by Cronos and the result was Chiron. When Philyra saw her child, she was horrified. She screamed out of despair, that she had given birth to a monster - because Chiron turns out to be half horse and half a divine being.*"

§ 58. The First Wound – Soul Loss

"*What is important for you to know, Heru, is that mixed creatures such as a centaur teach us important knowledge about the nature of our soul. Chiron teaches us that the inner nature of human beings consists of two opposite qualities. The horse symbolizes your animal side, and the humanoid part is the divine part. The challenge that every human being faces on the road towards illumination is to become a skilled horse rider who has the animal part under conscious control."*

"In all his behavior you can observe that Chiron suffers from a severe wound. Because of the way he is conceived, as an unwanted child and the result of adultery, his mother expels him. This is his First Wound, the wound that causes the nature of 'The Decent'. Remember your own Descent, Heru. You fell from Heaven as the result of the poisoning of the profane world, caused by King Herla. Chiron's First Wound is caused by the rejection of his mother. This causes a split between his horse part and his divine self. His mother is so startled by his strangeness that she repels him: she abandons her child from pure shame and disgust. The rejection of his mother causes the First Wound in Chiron. He feels cast out by the gods, he feels rejected in spite of his divine origin. It hurts him deeply, and this hurt results in a severe case of soul loss: this soul loss causes Chiron to become unpredictable. He behaves untamed and is extremely sensitive."

But Chiron is a centaur with extraordinary talents that make him the wisest and justest of all the Centaurs. He is openhearted, docile, and sensible, this is in contrast to the other Centaurs who are hateful, wild and thoughtless. Poor Chiron is abandoned by both his father and his mother. But because of his talents and his divine heritage, Chiron catches the attention of the Sun and the Moon, and they decide to raise him."

In spite of Chiron's tempestuous and untamed nature, he is very sensible! The gods and goddesses love him dearly. Apollo, the Sun God, and Diana, the Moon Goddess decide to train him in their specialties. Apollo teaches the young centaur the art of medicine, herbs, music, archery, hunting, gymnastics and prophecy. He makes him rise above his beastly nature. This is the reason why Chiron becomes famous for his knowledge and his skills with medicine. He knows everything there is to know about botany and pharmacy, the science of herbs and medicine. Diana shares her knowledge of weaponry with him and her knowledge about wild and untamed animals. Chiron invents the bow; he develops into a talented musician and a skilled hunter. Chiron unfolds all his talents and becomes famous, he isn't just an instructor; he develops into a great teacher, a philosopher, and a hermit. This is the nature of the great creature we will be meeting in this cave, Heru. An excellent opportunity to consult this great healer about the illness of the Wounded King."

§ 59. The Second Wound – The Wounded Healer

I walk with Idris along the sunny path in the direction of the Cave of Chiron. Idris tells me that heroes from all over the world come to visit Chiron. Achilles, Jason, and even the great healer Asclepius. All have visited Chiron to be taught. I carry a small barrel of wine with me as a gift for Chiron. I hope to drink a glass of wine with him. But wine belongs to all Centaurs together. At the moment I open the barrel, they come from all directions, drawn by the smell of the wine. When they discover that a barrel of wine has been opened, all the Centaurs gallop to Chiron's home and demand to know why Chiron has opened the wine without asking for their permission.

The Centaurs crowd around me, Idris, and Chiron. They threaten us. This turns out to be a huge disaster, several of the Centaurs try to scare me away. They gallop towards me, prancing and snorting, ordering me to *'never come back'*. Chiron does not participate in the quarrel. He keeps close by and keeps an eye on the whole crisis as it escalates. The Centaurs start to fight because of the unfairness. They push and pull me to chase me away. I feel terribly threatened, I feel the need to defend myself. I take my bow and arrow, and start shooting around in a wild way to keep myself safe. Arrows, stones, spears fly around in one big chaos. In this fight, in this chaos, Chiron is wounded by one of my poisoned arrows... and this type of poison causes fatal injuries because the points of my arrows are doused in the deadly venom of King Herla's poisoned drink. Chiron is in excruciating pain and anguish! There is no medication that can ease this infliction.

Chiron is desperate. How to heal this wound? Maybe by using the herb Centaurida? Because the flower of this herb causes pain to disappear. Chiron smears an ointment made of these flowers on his limbs. I hear him singing a magical hymn, so enchantingly beautiful! It is a song straight from the stars. He sings it in an enchanting voice, and in this way, he is able to stop the flow of blood from his wounded side. But although the blood flow stops, the wound does not heal.

Immediately, I have to think about the wound of the Wounded King. Is the nature of his wound similar to the wound of Chiron? What lesson can be learned here? Normally, a wound infected by King Herla's poison would be fatal. Chiron perishes from the pain, but he cannot heal himself. I sigh in despair. *"I wish I had water from the Fountain of Life, then I could poor this pain-reducing water on your wound. This magical water is even capable of returning the lost part of your soul to you."*

Chiron is tortured by the pain, but being the son of the gods, he is immortal! Even death cannot set him free from this pain. I am desperate, how do I solve this drama that I caused? I feel responsible and guilty. Suddenly, I think of Eternity. She has appeared at odd moments, and offers great advice. I decide to call out for her help.

I call out for the Great One who rules the Land of Shadows
She who lives in the Past, the Present, and the Future
I follow your footsteps through the Enchanted Land
Whisper the wisdom of Immortality, Eternity

...Then I hear her, voice crystal, clear her thoughts form in my head. "*Heru, the only solution for Chiron is to switch places with Prometheus. The wound can only heal when you realize that*

The Wound is the Place where the Light enters you.[3]

Idris comments: *"Prometheus lives in the Underworld; he is punished because he stole fire from Heaven. If we need Heavenly Light to cure Chiron's wound, we need to visit the realms of the subconscious mind to obtain the Light in the Darkness."*

And thus, my visit to the Cave of Sagittarius takes another turn. Idris and I leave the sunny island, followed by the by pain-overwhelmed Chiron. I am fully aware that I caused a dramatic situation, and I should solve it. When we are back ashore, we find a cave that gives access to the Underworld. At the entrance of the cave hang two torches. We each take a torch and descend into the dark, eerie realms of the subconscious mind.

After a long walk through a dark corridor, I find Prometheus, chained to a rock. I am puzzled by his situation. I try to understand why he has been punished so severely by the gods. "*Why did you steal fire from the Gods, Prometheus? Do you feel chained to the earth?*

Then I hear the voice of Eternity. "*Prometheus has been punished because time and again he tries to solve problems by finding a physical solution, instead of a spiritual one. This*

[3] Jalal ad-Din Rumi

is what stealing fire from the Gods means: by stealing fire from the Gods, one gets access to knowledge that you are not capable of applying in the right way. As a punishment, Prometheus is chained to a rock in the Underworld. That rock is the Earth herself. But meanwhile, the Earth is also the Altar of the Gods."

§ 60. Aquila the Eagle

"Prometheus can only be liberated when an Immortal is willing to take his place. This would mean that the Immortal loses his immortality and will eventually die. Prometheus is also in a hopeless situation. Chained to the rock of matter, he is visited by an eagle every day. Aquila descends from heaven and picks a portion of his liver. This causes him immense pain. When it gets dark, the liver grows back... only to be consumed by the eagle the next day once again. Chiron decides to take the offer and take the place of Prometheus and to give up his immortality.

I observe the situation filled with guilt, because this entire situation is caused by me, by my poisonous arrow. Every day the eagle comes to pick Chiron at the open wound. But Aquila is not an ordinary eagle. It is the Holy Spirit himself. I watch Chiron's pain, his torture, his powerlessness, and inability to lift his soul. I see him tearing at his chains in unbearable pain. I witness how the eagle pecks around in the open wound of his soul loss. Aquila flies with Chiron's liver, with his life force, in the direction of the Sun. Aquila is the eagle of past time and space. He the bird of immortality. He is the bringer of the secrets beyond the soul. For matter is just a vehicle in which the soul can manifest. Finally, the three goddesses of fate cut off Chiron's life thread. Finally, he is freed from his incurable wound.

Eternity still observes the scene. She decides to grant Chiron a resting place in the heavens. She comes down to lift him up to the heavenly realm. There, She prepares a place for him, to shine in the night sky as the constellation Sagittarius, the Archer. At the moment Chiron takes this place, he becomes the horse-man – the transformed human being. He is freed from the Wheel of Reincarnation and finally enters the spiritual world for eternity.

After this, Eternity speaks to me again. I hear her whispers in my mind. "*What about you, Heru? You are the Sun hero, the Soul of Light. Yes, I am talking to you! Can you pass the Eagle's test? Can you transform your First Wound? Also, you fell from Heaven. Also, you were also abandoned by the Gods. Can you connect with the Light of the Sun and Moon?*"

I answer her; *"I have been wandering through the Underworld, wondering: Where in the surrounding woodlands must I search to heal my wound? Where do I find the herb Centaurida, so that I can put the flower of no-pain on my limbs? How can I return safely and alive from the Underworld wherefrom no one returns! What magic hymn can help me? What song from the stars can I chant, to stop the flow of blood from my wounded side? I search the fountain of life, so that I can pour its pain-stilling waters on my limbs.*

Can those pain stilling-waters of the Fountain of Life heal my wound and even bring back my soul again?"

Then I become aware of the voice of the Eagle. "*Heru, you need to fly! Fly on, fly higher, and place yourself on the arrow of Chiron. Let him shoot your Spirit upwards. Use your bow – the Moon – and your arrow – Sagitta. Fly in spirit upwards higher than the rainbow. What arrow should Chiron use? Do you give him the poisonous arrow that injured you in your thigh? That same arrow that cripples you? Remember that the wound can only heal when you realize that:*

The Wound is the Place where the Light enters you.[4]

Fly into the heavens on the arrow that caused your second wound and search for the Centaur's herb that grows next to the Fountain of Life, by shooting your spirit upwards towards the stars."

---

[4] Jalal ad-Din Rumi

§ 61. Cygnus the Swan

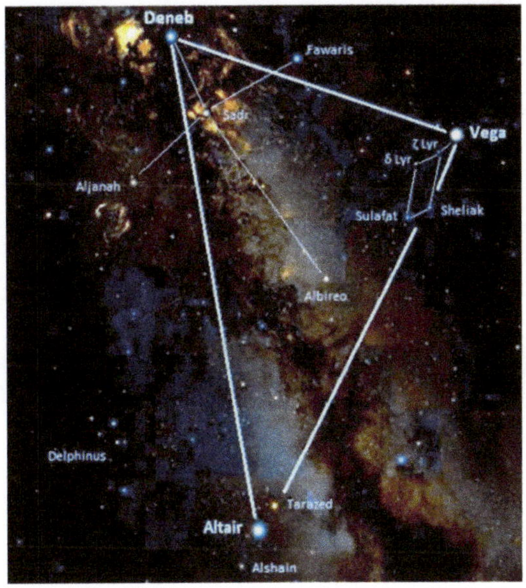

I fly upwards on the poisonous arrow. I pass the clouds; stars shoot around me. I fly into the direction of the Polestar. Suddenly, I feel how yet another bird is circling around me. It is Cygnus, the celestial swan. Watch how Cygnus circles upwards in slow circles, upwards around my spine. The constellation Cygnus is shaped like a cross. I clearly hear the voice of Cygnus whispering in my ear: *"I am the soul crucified on the Cross of Elements. Heal your soul of its incurable wound, fly arrow, fly higher, rise upwards into the sky."*

§ 62. Lyrae, the Vulture

Eternity witnesses everything that happens. She knows how deplorable you feel. *"Heru, your task has not been finished yet. Rise even higher on the back of Sagitta. Can you hear the music? Listen to your mother, the Moon. See her arch in front of you. Witness how the legacy you got from your mother, the Huntress, merges with the gifts from your father. Watch how the archer's bow turns into a harp with seven strings."*

"Apollo's lyre sounds through the entire Universe and plays the music of the spheres, watch the seven classical planets, each playing one of the strings. Up, fly up. You fly even higher in the direction of music from the harp. Do you see the heavenly harp in front of you? A beautiful shining constellation in the heavens. When you approach it, it comes to life and shapeshifts into the Vulture, the Eternal Mother, keeper of the Seven Secrets of Death. Her celestial home is in the constellation Lyrae. Listen to her message: "I am Eternal Justice. I bring a God's judgment, and give birth to your life in Heaven. The solution to your First Wound is to build your internal heaven."

"Here in Sagittarius, it becomes obvious that one of the major underlying themes that cause friction is that of Direction. Heru, you need to realize that we human beings are all Centaurs, half animal, half divine. We live on planet earth surrounded by Satyrs, people who are driven by their desires. We try to get control over our issues. The First Wound – is caused by the fact that we have fallen from heaven. We are challenged to make the best of our lives in the world of matter. The Archer is the divine part of our inner nature. This part of ourselves is the horse rider that guides our animal self – the horse - towards some one specific objective by shooting the arrow into the direction of heaven. The archer sends his arrow towards a desired point; he aims at a specific goal. This sense of direction or guidance is the Great Work of self-expression and expansion of consciousness. Choose your goals, Heru, choose them wisely. Let yourself be led by Beauty, Wonder, and Mystery!"

While I marvel at these last words, I hear the voice of Idris, who summons me to return to the Great Hall. He pulls me by the sleeves of my coat and urges me to follow him. From the sky, a leaf swirls down. No, it is not a leaf, it is twinkling! It is the next shard of the Mirror of Heaven that swirls downwards. I pluck it out of thin air and notice that on this shard is depicted the image of the Guardian of the Rainbow.

"Take it with you to the Hall of the Round Table Heru", Idris remarks. We are back at the door, and walk into the Great Hall.

I immediately walk towards the Wounded King. I bend over him and I tell him;

"The wound can only heal when you realize that:

The Wound is the Place where the Light enters you.

We all need to take responsibility for how we feel and consciously fill our lives with Beauty, Wonder and Mystery! Only then can we heal ourselves; only then can we become the Ruler of our Inner Kingdom."

The Wounded King nods his head in appreciation. *"I appreciate the mystery that you share with me, the achieved wisdom of your latest adventure. It helps me to soften the pain, but it does not heal the Wound, Heru."*

"Then I will continue my adventure and remain in search of a remedy for your wound."

The Golden Ring in Autumn

If you want to learn more about the myths belonging to the three tarot cards of the autumn season, look at the website. In the shop you find several video programs to deepen your knowledge even more:

https://www.hermeticartsandsciences.org/product/video-course-the-golden-ring-in-autumn-tarot-journey-4/

In the making are The Otherworldly Autumn of Murias, and the Tapestries of the Goddess in Libra, Scorpio and Sagittarius.

♑ DAIMON EST DEUS INVERSUS ע

Trump XV – Capricorn

Daimon est Deus Inversus

The Child of the Forces of Time, Lord of the Gates of Matter

Hebrew letter	**Ayin ע**
meaning	**Eye**
Simple letter	**Mirth**
Path color	**Indigo**
Sign	**Capricorn ♑**

Thirty-Two Paths of Wisdom:

The Twenty-sixth Path is called the Renovating Intelligence, because the Holy god renews by it all the changing things which are renewed by the creation of the world.

§ 63. The Cave of the Opposer

I tap with my Batocchio and sit down in my meditation chair, and I project myself into the Hall of the Round Table. As usual, the Wounded King lies on his bed. He is surrounded by a group of ladies dressed in white, who all carry items to heal his wound. One lady carries a bowl of water, the next a towel, and the third lady holds the twigs of the famous herb Centaurida; they take care of the wound. I look into the Wounded King's eyes, and his eyes are broken. I see his pain. I ask him whether his wound has improved. He tells me that he has less pain, but the inflammation is still severe. With a sigh, I release the air from my lungs. *"I will keep trying to find a cure for you, my dear king. That is why I am here. I am eager to learn what kind of healing is hidden behind the next stained-glass door."*

As usual, I walk around the Round Table. Then the mist forms in the center of the hall, and Idris steps forward from the cloud. He greets me in his usual way and tells me that I will visit the constellation Capricorn, and we both circumambulate the Round Table to check the shards of the Mirror of Heaven, the image of the Guardian of the Rainbow shows itself on the table. The band of gold has grown again. It starts in Aries and has reached the door of Capricorn now.

I look in the direction of the next door, and read the title of the Cave: *'Deus est Demon Inversus'*. My eyebrows rise, and the hairs on my arms stand upright. I am super alert now, and adrenaline rushes through my veins. Idris and I now walk towards the stained-glass door. Idris turns his head towards me and remarks: *"Make yourself ready for a bumpy ride, Heru!"*

I take a good look at the door in front of me, and I see how it opens slowly. I feel the handle in my hand and press it. I feel how the door opens and I hear strange sounds. When I have opened the door fully, I find myself at the edge of the Universe. What a strange cave this is! In front of me, dark space stretches out endlessly. The darkness is lit with tiny sparkling stars. At my feet, I see the outlines of a glittering path of stars. Carefully, I put my foot on the path to try out whether the path is able to carry my weight. I carefully place first one foot, and then the other on the path. I start to walk the stellar path; it takes me into the center of the Universe. Slowly, it takes me upwards, turning like a spiral. I turn around and see how the door, which leads towards my normal consciousness, gets smaller and smaller as I walk deeper into the Universe.

Slowly, I walk the stellar path. I notice that Idris has now taken the shape of a black dog again. He walks in front of me, and he shows me where to go. I follow him. We walk endlessly in the direction of the center, and when we do that, we also walk back in time. When we reach the center, we take a seat in the first ring of stars that encircles the beginning of the Universe. Then I hear a familiar voice: *"Welcome, Heru. You are invited to witness a spectacle. You will witness an extraordinary part of history that is about to take place here. Look in that direction — that is the center of the Universe."* I am surprised by what I see. I see a big egg.

"Yes," the voice of Eternity echoes in my mind. *"The Universe is a huge egg built of... nothingness. Let me tell you the story of the creation of the Universe. Before the beginning of time, there was a Sea of Nothingness, of no-thing-ness! There were no things yet, there was no matter! The Sea of No-thing-ness is perfect in its Unity and At-oneness. Amidst this Sea of Consciousness, I, the Great Goddess Eternity, become conscious of myself. I become aware of myself in this center of perfectness, where No-Thing happens. Absolutely No-Thing. This lasts an Eternity because here, time does not exist yet. In this endless Eternity of Nothingness and Perfectness, I become conscious of myself. My secret name is 'The Becoming One, The Beginning'... but still No-thing happens. I am the One, the Creatrix. I turn inwards, and I conclude that I want to Know Myself. But I am the Only One that exists... and after an Eternity of Silence in Perfectness, I decide that I might evolve when I divide myself into little pieces. In this way, it would be possible that one piece of myself could interact with another piece of myself, and then movement, experience, and evolution would become possible. So, I turn inwards to brood on this idea."*

§ 64. The Oldest Spark

"I talk with all my potentialities, which are all still a part of my Unity. One aspect of myself I call the Oldest Spark. I talk with the Oldest Spark about the idea of dividing myself into pieces. The answer from the Oldest Spark is: 'We will lose the Perfectness, because the Unity is lost. Then we will have diversification'. I turn inside and I realize

that it is not possible to experience, to cause movement and evolution without losing my Oneness. This is only possible when a part of myself cuts itself loose from my Oneness. That would mean that my Perfectness would not be quite perfect any longer. I contemplate and exchange with the part of me whom I call the Oldest Spark about how to do this and what would be needed."

"The Oldest Spark answers that he is prepared to make that sacrifice — to be separated from the Perfectness — but that, in the meantime, a Way Back has to be created, because all parts must be united into One again at the end of this Cosmic Day. All experiences of all facets of the Unity must be reabsorbed into the Whole. "We need a thrust block at the other side of creation," the Oldest Spark argues. "This will cause all the parts that will be split off to push themselves off from the bottom — at the Nadir of their existence — and bounce back, and thus return to the Unity.""

"I meditate deeply about all these ideas, and I think that this would be the perfect solution. I meditate on all aspects of myself. I connect with Space, with Moisture, with Fire, with all my aspects, about how to go along with this. And I conclude that if the Oldest Spark needs a thrust block to make the Way Back possible, then one of my parts must take this task upon itself. That part of me would be divided from the Perfectness and would become the opposing force against whom everybody would fight."

"I ask all the aspects of my Unity which part would be prepared to take this task upon itself. The Oldest Spark has had time to think this through, and he says that he is prepared to be the sacrifice. 'I want to be the sacrifice. But under one condition: I want to have children — I want to have an estate of four children. Through me, through my sacrifice, the manifested Universe will be created, and I want that via my four Children, the Way Back will come into manifestation.'"

"Oldest Spark, you are an aspect of my heart," I say. "You are a wise being. Your light is seen in the Highest Realms of the Universe. You will always be able to fly high enough to unify yourself with me, even when I cut you loose from me. Like an ox, you will lack one essential piece of your body as a token of the offering you gave. You will separate yourself from me, so that in the Perfectness is built in a little piece of imperfection — exactly enough imperfection to cause the diversification of the All."

"The Oldest Spark nods his head. 'This is exactly what is needed. The Oneness will always be One, but because of this Imperfection, which is still a part of the Oneness and Perfectness, the diversification will take place, and the Universe will come into manifestation — a place of Beauty, Wonder, and Mystery! From this Universe, stars will be born. The Gods will come into manifestation, and with the Gods an unending number of worlds will be created and will become the home of living beings. Through these beings, Eternity will be able to experience Herself. They will all be a part of you, Eternity, and the sum will be you. In this way, you will be both Immanent and Transcendent. But

if I cut myself loose from you, I become your Opposer: I will become the thrust block. I will form a firm base whereon and through which everything will be able to unify itself with you again. But, Eternity, you have to understand what this means to me! This will change me — I will become something entirely different. I want to make this sacrifice, but still cause unity. This is the reason why I want to have sons!'"

§ 65. The Four Princes

I take a look into the Mirror of the Heavens, I mirror myself in the Waters of Reflection, and I answer the Oldest Spark: "Your wish will be granted. If you sacrifice yourself, four sons will be born. They will be born from the Mother Goddess. They will always be visible in the Cosmic Waters. Ursa Major, the Great Bear, will—like the hand of a cosmic clock—indicate which one of the Four Brothers will rule. They will each rule one season."

"They will encircle the place where, from my birth channel, I will create the entire Cosmos. They will be dancing around the place from where every Polestar will shine—forever. Here your sacrifice will be honored. From the Polestar, the Little Bear encircles my Birth Channel. The Great Bear will serve as a heavenly pointer towards the Four Sons. The Four Elements will come into manifestation at the highest level. Every element will be channeled by one of the Sons and their Mother. They will be honored in all cultures. The Jewish tradition will call them Chaioth Ha Kodesh. The Christian tradition will call them the Four Evangelists. The Egyptians will call them the Four Sons."

The Oldest Spark thinks long, and at the end, he nods in agreement. The Oldest Spark and Eternity embrace each other, and then they separate. When they do this, an enormous cosmic explosion is heard—the Big Bang: an enormous outburst of fire and energy, the first sound ever heard. The Oldest Spark leaves the Heavens, and at that exact moment that he does so, he changes into... King Herla. He falls—head down—out of the Heavens, passes through the surface of the Earth, and drills himself right through all the layers of the Inner Earth, until he has reached the deepest point in the Inner Earth. There, he builds his castle, where he brews his potions and creates magical spells. His talents make him a startling necromancer. He names his enchanted castle the Castle of Marvels.

At the moment King Herla reaches the Nadir of his Descent, the starry Heavens come into being. The stars together create a star mirror that covers the entire Enchanted Lands. They create a lapis lazuli-blue dome, sparkling with lights. The stars collect all the Wisdom of the Unity of the Cosmos, and together they form a stellar clock that indicates what Caves will become active during a period of time and dictate fate for all who live on the planet. At that very moment, matter is born, and around the Polestar, four Goddesses give birth to the Four Princes, the Sons of the Oldest Spark:

- The Queen of Air gives birth to the star Fomalhaut, the fish who jumps out of the water bucket of the constellation Aquarius. This Royal Star becomes the Ruler of the Magical Winter of the Land of Falias.

- The Queen of Earth gives life to the star Aldebaran, the blaze on the forehead of the Heavenly Bull. This Royal Star becomes the Ruler of the Enchanting Spring of the Land of Gorias.

- The Queen of Fire gives life to the star Regulus, the heart of the Heavenly Lion. This Royal Star becomes the Ruler of the Spellbinding Summer of the Land of Findias.

- And finally, the Queen of Water gives life to the star Antares, the heart of the Heavenly Scorpion. This Royal Star becomes the Ruler of the Otherworldly Autumn of the Land of Murias.

Four Goddesses, who are located behind the veil of matter and time, weave a honeycomb of light—a honeycomb of light that they call the Clothes. 'The Clothes' is the name they give to the woven Primeval Matter of Light and the energy with which all matter is built. At the very moment of creation, when the Oldest Spark descends into his fate, at that very same moment, there also happens a miracle in the star sign of Capricorn. Look there, Heru, you can see the Sea Goat jumping from the Heavens. It is the Oldest Spark who transforms himself into King Herla. Precisely at the moment that he leaves the cosmic ocean of primordial water and Unity; the First Matter is formed. Through the four Elemental Queens, the Four Sons are born—the Four Princes—and the entire birth process of Creation starts. I, Eternity, create primeval matter, and from this, the Four Elemental Queens weave the Four Enchanted Lands. They weave everything into existence, giving birth to all the gods. The Enchanted Lands become filled with plants, animals, and human beings. Because of the sacrifice of King Herla, matter becomes possible, and the First Time comes into being.

I am dizzy because of this flood of information. Idris and I still sit at the border of the circle of light at the edge of the Cosmos. I am completely aware of the fact that the story I have seen unfolding is not ancient history, but an ongoing process. Idris and I have watched the principle of creation here. I see a glittering shard whirling towards me.

"Catch that thing," Idris says. *"This is the shard that represents the image of this cave. It is the tarot card Demon est Deus Inversus; this means that King Herla is God upside down."*
Then Idris rises, and he reaches out a hand to me to help me up. *"It is time for us to go back to our own time and space."*

In my imagination, I rise from my cosmic seat, and Idris and I walk back to the tiny point of light in the distance, where our conscious minds and our bodies are resting and waiting at the Hall of the Mountain King. We walk back over the spiral path to the place from where we came. We walk through the stained-glass door and arrive in the hall, where the Wounded King waits for us. He is eager to learn what insights and healing capacities we have gained from this journey. *"Welcome, Heru. You made quite a spectacular journey. What did you learn this time?"*

I draw a deep breath, and then I start to talk: *"I have learned that the Opposer is an inevitable part of Creation. King Herla may seem harsh and evil, but he has an important task in the scheme of evolution. King Herla taught me that materialism, idolatry, and distraction from spiritual growth are the forces that hold me imprisoned in the profane materialistic world. I have learned that I am constantly drawn into a struggle between worldly desires and spiritual purposes. I can also fall myself when I let myself become tempted by pride or when I rebel against higher principles. I can reach my personal nadir when I let myself become seduced by primitive desires. I can become enchanted by King Herla by seeking power or success at the cost of my spiritual light, and thus become a trickster myself who disrupts my environment."*

I sigh and turn inwards. What gift can I give the king? I approach his sickbed and sit down next to him. I take his hand and tell him: *"'Demon est Deus Inversus'. Look at your wound again, my dear king. When King Herla hurts you, he also challenges you to become even stronger than you were. Do not fear him when he touches your life, but see it as an opportunity to grow."*
Then I hear Idris' voice again: *"It is time to return to the profane world, Heru. It is time to reconnect with your physical body..."*

Then I see my physical body sitting in my meditation room. I fly towards it and stand in front of it. Then I sit down in my body. When I am back in the Here-and-Now, I lift my altar light, and in a spontaneous outcry I recite:

Holy art Thou, Creatrix of the Universe
Holy art Thou, whom nature has not formed
Holy art Thou, oh vast and mighty one
Creatrix of Light and Darkness

I feel fully energized and happy. I stretch my muscles, move my neck, I breathe consciously in and out, and I return to the Here-and-Now, feeling great and refreshed.

XVII ♒ THE OCEAN MOTHER

Trump XVII – Aquarius ♒

The Ocean Mother

The Ocean Mother – The Daughter of the Firmament – The Dweller between the Waters

Hebrew letter	**Tzaddi צ**
Meaning	**Fish Hook**
Simple Letter:	**Imagination**
Path color	**Violet**
Sign	**Aquarius ♒**

Thirty-Two Paths of Wisdom:

The Twenty-eight Path is called the Natural Intelligence, and it is so called because through it is consummated and perfected the Nature of every existing thing beneath the Sun.

§ 66. The Cave of the Ocean Mother

I tap with my Batocchio and sit down in my meditation chair, and I project myself into the Hall of the Round Table. As usual, the Wounded King lies on his bed, in deep contemplation of his own shadow. I ask the king if he has accepted his fate, and the King answers: *"Acceptance is a heavy chain, Heru. I wear it, yet my heart still yearns to stand tall and proud. My illness offers me strange opportunities. I am momentarily in an interesting dialogue with the other part of myself, King Herla. This enables me to take responsibility for all my feelings instead of putting the blame on someone else. The strange thing is that this means I get more power over my own feelings, and it enables me to control my pain. But it does not heal my wound."*

"Then I will continue my journey, my dear king. I am eager to learn what information and healing the next shard of the Mirror of Heaven will reveal. I am ready to travel through the lands beyond the next stained-glass door."

As usual, I walk around the Round Table. I look in the direction of the next door and read the title of the Cave: *'The Ocean Mother'*.

Idris appears in his usual unique way, and he takes me to the next door. *"The location of this Tarot card is the place of Creation. We will enter the Enchanted Lands in the First Time, immediately after the Creation and the Great Flood. There is a connection between the Stars of Heaven and the splashing waterfalls, the fast-flowing rivers, and the lovely streams, which appear throughout the entire Tarot deck,"* Idris remarks.

The stained-glass door opens, and on the other side, the entrance is flanked by two sycamore trees. Idris starts to talk and explain the scene we are entering. *"These two sycamore trees are an ancient symbol that marks the entrance of a sacred place. The sycamore tree is the symbol of the wisdom rooted in the heavens. Follow me, and I will guide you through this Cave."*

Then I hear a soft giggle from a woman's voice. I find myself surrounded by a deep blue night sky. I hear the soft sound of streaming water; I discover a river in front of me. I walk towards the shore. In front of me, a boat is waiting. It is an ancient sailing ship. The boatman greets us and invites us aboard the ship. He raises the sail. When we are onboard the ship, it starts to move in the direction of the north. We sail over the river, and we can clearly see a desert landscape on both sides of the river. Directly behind a small border of palm trees and dry bushes, the dry shore's sand dunes rise up, giving access to the endless desert.

I ask the sailor where is taking us. He answers that we are going in the direction of the West. *"The direction of the Setting Sun is the area where the entrance of the Underworld is located. The Underworld is the mysterious area of our subconscious mind. It is a fluid world where all the psychic vibrations and forms of consciousness take shape in the mind."*

Suddenly, the boat goes downward. It enters into the mouth of a Cave. The blue night sky now changes into deep black darkness. *"Do not be afraid," the sailor says. "It will not stay dark for long. I will paddle you to the shore now. In a few minutes, His Majesty the Sun will enter into the Underworld and illuminate the Cave."*

Idris explains: *"Heru, we have now entered into the invisible world that is behind the scenes. Here, everything that is created comes forward from the Unmanifested Subconsciousness of Divinity. That makes this place awkward and unpredictable."*

The Goddess of the Firmament hovers over the scene of the creation myth. Her legs and arms are the pillars that uphold the Roof of Heaven. The Four Cardinal Directions, symbolized by the Four Sons of King Herla, provide her a solid ground to put her hands and feet on. In this way, the heavens are raised from the Celestial Waters and dry land appears.

We sail into the cave, and the landscape changes; the river leads us into a vast ocean. Above my head, I see an endless quantity of stars. In the center of the ocean, I see a pyramid protruding from the Deep Waters.

§ 67. The First Time

Idris comments: *"Heru, we have entered the First Time – the time of Creation, the time when everything is exactly as it should be. Look at the pyramid surrounded by the primordial waters; this is the first Dry Land of Creation. Look above your head. Do you see the Star Goddess? Her head is in the West, and her legs are in the East. She is the Milky Way. Her title is 'Ocean Mother' because she is the one who rules the Deep Oceans without and within. The Milky Way is the visible manifestation of the mysteries which she veils, because she herself is the Veil. She is the Veil of Light and of Cosmic Energies which clothe the Invisible Consciousness of the Eternal Mind."*

Now I feel a sphere of expectation building around me. Snakes, baboons, and jackals gather together at the entrance of the Cave. Then the baboons start to applaud and shriek. The Sun enters into the Underworld. The Sun travels on a majestic boat in the company of the most powerful and oldest gods. The Sun is followed by a procession of goddesses who wear a crown with a star on their heads. The sailor whispers to me that these are the Hour Goddesses; they are the Mistresses of the Decans, the proclaimers of Time in the Night. It is a magnificent sight! The procession of the Star Goddesses is followed by a large procession of smaller stars.

Together they create a procession of lights, which strides with great dignity through the night. Together they create a Serpent of Light. The procession of lights is so numerous and grand that the Snake of Light wraps the entire process of Creation in its endless coils. The Serpent of Light clothes all the invisible forces of the subconscious in the Light of Creation. In this way, the Serpent of Light encircles the entire space around the Celestial Globe: the inside is the visible light of manifestation; the outside consists of anti-matter in the Unmanifested.

§ 68. The Quarrel between Earth and Heaven

Then I hear two voices quarreling; two primordial gods are arguing fiercely. The God of Matter quarrels with the Ocean Mother. He is very angry with her and accuses her of eating her children. He even calls her names; he calls her *'Sow, who eats her piglets.'*

Idris asks for my attention: *"I have brought you here because you will get important information from their quarrel. It will reveal some of the Mysteries of the Universe, and it will give you access to the Wisdom of the Stars. Listen very carefully. Maybe you will not be able to understand everything that is explained to you here, but things will fall into place in time. Let these ideas fall into your mind like fertile seeds. They will start to take root, and you will be able to harvest the fruits of these ideas at a later date."*

Now the Ocean Mother and the God of Matter are quarreling so loudly that it even attracts the attention of their father. Their father is the God of Space. He speaks to the God of Matter and tells him not to be angry at his wife for eating her young: *"Be quiet, God of*

Matter. Your children shall live, and they shall be born in her birthplace in the East every day, in the same way that she gives birth to the Sun daily."

And while the God of Space says this, he lifts the Ocean Mother up, high into the sky. When the God of Space does that, the God of Matter becomes visible to my inner eye. I can clearly see him lying on the earth. He is covered with green vegetables, sheaves of corn, and fruit.

Now the sailor takes the floor again and explains to me what I see: *"Our ship has entered into the body of the Goddess of the Night. She is the Ocean Mother, the Goddess of the Deep. The Sun God, the Hour Goddesses, and all the stars of the Firmament enter into the Ocean Mother at the place of her head in the West. When His Majesty the Sun sets in the Western Horizon, all the stars of the Universe enter into the Mouth of the Ocean Mother."*

Now I can clearly hear what the Ocean Mother replies to the God of Matter, in answer to his remarks. She says: *"The stars travel to the boundaries of the sky — outside of me — in the night. Then you can see them, and they shine. During the day, they are inside me, and they cannot be seen. They enter into me and journey into the depths. I am the Mother of the Gods. I have not been called by this name since I gave birth to them. The Gods are in me and travel through me. I am Heaven. The Gods cannot fall because I hold them inside me. But they go down into the earth. There they die and enter into the Unconscious*

Realms. All who die go there; they go into the depths of the House of the God of Matter in the Earth. There they are purified for seventy days."

"As long as they are in the House of the God of Matter, in the Inner Earth, their names may not be named. Their names cannot be spoken aloud during that time. They undergo a purification. Their impurities are absorbed by the Earth. They are purified by the Earth, and the Earth loves them."

"They become pure, and they still live! The bodies of the gods are beheaded, and their heads are placed in the East! Their heads change and become shining stars. The stars are the heads of the gods! When they arrive in the East, a feast is celebrated. All the sins that they have committed have been absorbed into the Inner Earth. The Inner Earth purifies all the dead souls from any evil they have done; the evil is absorbed by the Earth, and the souls can continue to develop themselves."

"The tears they shed during the purification process become fish in the Underground River. Here in the river, deep down in the Underworld, the life of a star begins. It begins in the Lake of Fire. The Lake of Fire is the Great Purification Realm. When the souls come forth from these waters, they fly upwards out of the sea, and they change their form. The souls become stars, and they rise up from the Underworld and fly into the sky."

This is what the Ocean Mother tells the God of the Earth. But the God of Matter still does not agree with the Ocean Mother. He is still fighting her. He does not agree and commands the Ocean Mother that the souls must be permitted to show their heads in the East – to come forth from the Earth again. The God of Matter is very angry. He even commands the gods and shouts: *"Put an end to the appearance of those crazy heads!"*

The God of Matter shouts so loudly that the gods stop bathing in the Lake of Fire and listen to what he has to say. They tell the God of Matter that they want to live. They want to live and show their heads. They explain to the God of Matter how they do this: and I stand in the middle of this quarrel and hear the arguments from all sides. The gods answer the God of Matter: *"We are buried, just like the men on Earth,"* say the gods.

The God of Matter looks, and he sees that the purification in the Inner Earth indeed takes place. When that purification process has been finished, the God of Matter sees how the souls go forth; they travel in the sky at night. They journey to the boundaries of the sky. They do exactly the same thing as the dying people on Earth!

Now the Ocean Mother answers the God of Matter, and she says: *"Look how the gods watch the Living Ones, and witness how the souls also change into stars. They make a journey and they shine – beautiful souls – as stars in the Hours of the Night. My husband, although I swallow them, the stars are still alive. Every star that comes forth from the Inner Earth travels until it arrives at my birthplace in the East. There they party every day; they celebrate the birth of the Sun and the birth of Heru, the Child of Light, who is born on the Earth plane. The stars are born from my womb every day. They are born at the same time I give birth to the Sun. All the deceased souls are reborn from me daily, just like the Sun."*

"Every star that has purified itself in the House of the God of Matter is called by its name in praise. It rises from the Inner Earth. A great party is held for them when they withdraw from the House of the God of Matter; the feast is organized because of the purification, together with the publication of the new name for the newly born soul. The name of a star is not pronounced until it rises from the House of the God of Matter. The name of the star that sets is not pronounced until it rises from the Underworld. So, do not quarrel with me because I eat my young, my dear God of Matter!"

I watch as the God of Matter silently ponders what the Ocean Mother has told him, and he stops quarreling. He is thinking out loud: *"The mother sow eats her piglets. The Ocean Mother eats her stars, the souls. All mother beasts are the same."*

Then the God of Space lifts the Ocean Mother. He supports her as he raises her high in the sky. Idris and I remain silent and observe the scene. Then I ask Idris: *"When I think about the dynamics between the God of Matter and the Ocean Mother, I'm starting to believe that the ancients believed in reincarnation?"*

"That absolutely is the case," Idris answers. *"That is also one of the reasons they considered physical death not to be the end, but the start of an interesting afterlife."*

Then I see the Sun sinking in the West again. The Sun God is on his way once more to be eaten by the Ocean Mother. I see how the God of Space lowers the Ocean Mother again toward the Earth, so that she and the God of Matter can make love once more. And the quarrel starts again. Because once again, the Ocean Mother eats her children. But then the Ocean Mother tells the God of Matter the real names of the stars; she calls them by their names; she calls them 'food'—that is how she tells us that stars are spiritual food.

Idris and I watch as the Ocean Mother swallows her living children. In the morning, they are reborn. Together with the Sun, they rise from the House of the God of Matter. We see them once again being swallowed. They enter the mouth of the Ocean Mother; they travel through her body during the day. The stars travel to the boundaries of Heaven, following the Sun in the day sky, illuminating the Beautiful Road in the night sky.

§ 69. The Cycle of Life and Death

I hear the voice of the Mother Goddess; she speaks to me personally to explain what I have seen: *"I, the Ocean Mother, give birth to the stars. On the Earth, people die and descend into the Underworld. They rest in the Underworld for seventy days to lose their impurity to the Inner Earth. After those seventy days, every soul becomes a Living Soul Flame and their new name is pronounced and proclaimed! This happens to every deceased soul of the Earth, and when the name of a deceased is pronounced after they have purified themselves, they become a living star and rise to the Heaven. Every deceased soul becomes a star."*

"Purified, every human soul comes into a new life and rises from the horizon like the star Sirius. They are purified, and after seventy days they show their shining heads in the East; their heads have become like the heads of the Gods. Watch the rising of the gods; the first gods we see rising are Orion and Sirius. After they have spent seventy days in the Underworld, they rise again in the sky as newborn stars."

"When a new head shows itself at the eastern horizon, another one disappears in the west. The bad qualities of the deceased souls are absorbed by the Inner Earth, and they purify themselves. They drop their tears, and these tears change into fish. In the Underworld, there are lakes and rivers. When their tears drop into the streams of the Underworld, the stars purify themselves in this way, and they take their fish form here. In this way, all the tears of the world create the Four Rivers of Purification that stream from the point of Creation downwards to purify the hearts of every man and woman."

§ 70. The Four Rivers

A river of tears streams downward,
towards the Enchanted Lands,
then the waters are divided into four streams
by Four Fairy Queens.

They water your Magical Garden;
The name of the first is the River of Growth,
also called the River between the Worlds,
which goes around all the land of Falias.

The name of the second river
is the River of Life and Light.
This river goes around all the Land of Gorias.

The name of the third river is the River of Fire,
of Courage and Love,
which waters the Land of Findias.

The fourth river starts from the Lake of Reflection
and is the River of Imagination.
This river waters the Land of Murias.

The Forces of Creation claim you, Heru.
They have put you in the Enchanted Lands
to develop your Magical Garden and take care of it.

Purify yourself in the four rivers that surround this sacred space.
They cleanse your experiences and perspective of the past.
Realize that the past has gone,
and your heart becomes purified from sorrows.

§ 71. The Four Fairy Queens

The Ocean Mother continues: "*Meet the Faery Queens who rule over the Elemental Waters that stream down from the highest point of Creation. The name of the first Elemental Queen is Titiana. She is the Queen of Air. With her magical wand, she draws the soul flames into the River between the Worlds, that waters the lands of Falias. The River Between the Worlds is the Northern River. This river flows downward from the highest mountain in the North, located at the edge between life and death, this river brings down awareness of the Inner Worlds."*

"The name of the second Elemental Queen is Melusine. She is the Queen of Water. She catches the Waters with her Cup and opens the Windows of Opportunities. Melusine directs these opportunities through the Lands of Murias. She rules over the River of Imagination and Re-memberance."

"The name of the third Elemental Queen is Hippolyte. She is the Queen of Fire. With her Sword, she directs the River of Fire, Courage, and Love into the Lands of Findias. Hippolyte nails every soul flame to their fate. The River of Fire is the Southern River. It brings love, passion, and the delight by which the work becomes beneficial and healthy."

"The name of the Fourth Elemental Queen is Queen Mab, Queen of the Inner Earth. With her magical dish that contains the fruits of the Earth, she rules over the River of Life and Light. She opens the opportunities to be born into a new life. The River of Life is the Eastern River; it is highly influenced by the Element of Earth. This is a river of growth and abundance. She brings awareness of the laws of growth."

"The River of Imagination is also the River of Dreams and Re-Memberance. New things can arise by using powerful imagination; the lessons learned in the past are essential for the success of the future."

Now Idris explains further. *"The Four Rivers of Purification are part of the Inner Landscape. They flow downward from the Mountaintops of the four Magical Countries – Falias, Gorias, Findias, and Murias – and bring blessings, healing, and inspiration to the Inner Kingdoms. They bring down blessings from Above, and they can be used to cleanse the Inner Landscape from blocked emotions, feelings, memories, and wounds. In the Enchanted Lands, they are connected to the four Queens."*

Then Idris offers me a bottle and instructs me to tap water from all the Four Rivers to heal myself and the Wounded King.

Then the sailor remarks that it is time to sail back my own time and place. The boatman now raises the sail. A strong wind starts to blow, and the sail curls and drifts in the direction of the South. I hear the sound of the splashing water. I think about the things that I have heard. I become aware of the fact that slowly it gets lighter. The sailor says that it is almost time for His Majesty the Sun to appear in the Eastern sky. I see the stars disappear slowly. In the back of my head, I hear the voice of the God of Matter: *"The Ocean Mother eats her children."*

The sailor tells me that we will now travel together with the deceased. Gods and souls travel together through the Earth realm of the Duat to purify themselves. In the Enchanted Land, the day starts. I feel a sensation of strong apprehension. In the trees, baboons gather. They watch the horizon. The sky is colored in beautiful red hues, and when the first rays of the sunlight touch the horizon, the baboons start to applaud. The birds start to sing; the winds start to blow. The sail catches the wind and brings me back into broad daylight. In the distance, I see two sycamore trees. Idris tells me that behind those trees my physical life will start again.

I pass the trees, and the boat docks at the stained-glass door of the Hall of the Round Table. I thank the sailor and ask his name. *"This is not the time to reveal my name to you, but you may think of me as the Ferryman."*

Then the sailor gives me a shard from the Mirror of Heaven. Clearly, I see the tarot image of the Ocean Mother reflected in it. The sailor waves goodbye, and I walk towards the Wounded King. I bow to the King and greet him. I show him the bottle with the mixture of the Four Rivers. *"What is it that you bring me this time, Heru?"*

"Oh, my dear King, I have learned that reincarnation is a fact and that in the Underworld all wounds are cured. The pain and the hurt feelings are purified in the Four Rivers of Purification. I have brought you a potion that contains all four the qualities. Drink from this Magical Potion, my dear King, and may your heart become purified and hale."

I give my healing potion to the King. He pours it into his wound and drinks a sip from the brew. He sighs. *"I really feel much better, Heru, not in the least because of your care and attention. But the Magical Potion cannot heal my wound."*

"Then my journey is not over," I assure the Wounded King.
I hear Idris's voice again. *"But it is enough for today, Heru. It is time to return to the profane world, Heru. It is time to reconnect with your physical body..."*

I see my physical body sitting in my meditation room. I fly towards it and stand in front of it. I sit in my body. When I am back into the Here-and-Now, I lift my altar light, and spontaneously I recite once again:

Holy art Thou, Creatrix of the Universe
Holy art Thou, whom nature has not formed
Holy art Thou, O vast and mighty one
Creatrix of Light and Darkness

I feel fully energized and happy. I stretch my muscles, move my neck, breathe consciously in and out, and return to the Here-and-Now, feeling great and refreshed.

XVIII
♓ THE MOON ROAD ק

Trump XVIII – Pisces ♓

The Moon Road

The Ruler of Flux and Reflux – The Child of the Sons of the Mighty

Hebrew letter	**Qoph ק**
Meaning	**Back of the Head**
Simple Letter:	**Sleep**
Path color	**Crimson (Ultra Violet)**
Sign	**Pisces**

Thirty-Two Paths of Wisdom:

The Twenty-ninth Path is the Corporeal Intelligence, so-called because it forms everybody which is formed beneath the whole set of worlds and the increment of them.

§ 72. The Cave of the Moon Road

I tap with my Batocchio and sit down in my meditation chair, and I project myself into the Hall of the Mountain King in the usual way. When I enter the great hall, the situation is unchanged. The Wounded King greets me. *"The water you brought me from those four rivers is magical. It cleanses and purifies me on different levels of my body and mind. I feel that my feelings of sin and shame are starting to dissolve, and I receive more understanding and insight into the entire situation as a result of this. I am gaining even more control over my own feelings, and my pain is dissolving. But my wound is not healed yet."*

"Then I will make the next journey, my dear King, on behalf of both you and myself. I have gained a lot of wisdom on these journeys, and the shards of the Mirror of Heaven cause incessant amazement in me. I am eager to travel through the Enchanted Lands beyond the next stained-glass door."

As usual, I walk around the Round Table. I look in the direction of the next door and read the title of the Cave: *"The Moon Road."*

Idris appears in his cloud of mist. Together, we walk to the next door. *"The location of this Tarot card is the Birth of the Light. In the Enchanted Lands, it is still the First Time."*

Idris taps with his wand on the next stained glass, the door opens, and I look into a landscape where a river flows from the West toward the East. It is utterly silent... There is no light except for the lights of the Eternal Stars, flickering in the far Above. I look upwards to see if I can recognize any of them. I notice the constellations Pisces and Perseus right above me. And exactly above the river shines the infamous star Algol.

§ 73. Algol

Then Idris starts to explain the situation we are in. *"Heru, it is important that you understand that the Tarot card of the Moon is not about the lunar powers, as many people think, but it is about the birth of the Inner Sun. The Moon that you see on the card is the waning moon that rises above the horizon at the place of Sunrise. At this particular time of the year, the waning Moon opens a pathway that the Sun can follow to be reborn at the end of its journey through the night."*

"The waning moon in Algol indicates where and when this pathway will open. When the waning moon is visible, you need to wait and observe the appearance of the Star of Venus as she rises before sunrise. Look here on the stained-glass door: Venus is symbolized by the geometrical figure that Venus makes around the Earth, the Pentagram. The Earth hovering in space in this image indicates that THIS is the place of Destiny. In opposition to many religions, Redemption does not take place in the Heaven Above, but in the Heaven Within and the Enchanted Lands around you."

In the distance, I see a procession approaching. I smell the scent of burning incense and I listen to the prayers they recite, an enchanting whispering echoes through the dark night. The priestesses are clothed in lapis lazuli-colored robes, adorned with sparkling stars, thus they blend into the landscape. Their faces are veiled. The priests are clad in long white robes. The procession of priests moves slowly and with dignity. They carry ritual staffs indicating their functions.

At a certain point in the landscape, I see two large hills rising at both sides of the river. Before the two hills, we stand still at a place where two jackals guard a passage. The two animals are sitting on top of two huge carved stones, facing each other. A female priest steps forward and declares that this is the shore of the Realm of Eternity, and that we are in between the Tides of Time, between Yesterday and Tomorrow.

I observe how the High Priestess leads the procession; she carries the wand of her office. At the northern side of the river, I spot a plateau. A staircase hewn into the rocks leads to this high place that overlooks the entire scene. The High Priestess climbs the staircase, followed by two priestesses. The entire company follows, one by one, climbing the steep and narrow staircase between the rocks. Idris and I follow at the end of the row.

We arrive at the plateau above the river, which overlooks the entire scene. There, the High Priestess takes her place, backing towards the north, facing the south. At both sides, one step behind her, the two priestesses walk in exactly the same rhythm. They carry staffs topped with moon symbols. Down below, through the valley, runs the river Urness, from West to East. Now the procession holds still. I watch how the High Priestess faces in the direction of the gate.

§ 74. Calling down the Moon

Everyone shifts their attention to the two hills and the gate that is guarded by the two jackals, toward the East. The High Priestess lifts up her arms. The entire landscape waits in expectation of what is coming next. I become aware of the sound of the waves, the moist air of the wild river, and the misty fog of splashing water. Then the High Priestess lifts her arms, and I hear her voice echoing over the waters. I get the shivers while I hear the Great Invocation of the Moon:

Goddess of the Night and of the Oceans
Blessed Queen of the Great Waters
She who creates the Mighty Images
She who controls the mighty forces with her powers

Show us Thy force and Thy might
Rise above the horizon, so that we can praise you
We welcome you as the waning moon,
you are the Crone, wise and full of power.

One of the priestesses' steps forward. On her head, she wears a ceremonial crown, depicting the Waning Moon. She takes her place in the East to mark the place where the Waning Moon will rise. Then the High Priestess continues her invocation of the Lunar Powers and addresses the priestess:

In your appearance of the Dark Moon
you are the mysterious Goddess of the Crossroads.
In your form of the New Moon
you take on your aspect of the mysterious waxing beauty.
In your form of the Full Moon
you take on your face of the mysterious Mirror of Reflection.
In your form of the Waning Moon,
you become the mysterious Giver of Wisdom.

Mighty Moon, open the Moon Road,

Show us the Way to the Birth of our Inner Sun!

Meanwhile, I realize that I am standing at the mouth of the River Urness, at the place where the Waters leave the Cave. I look at the two large hills rising at both sides of the

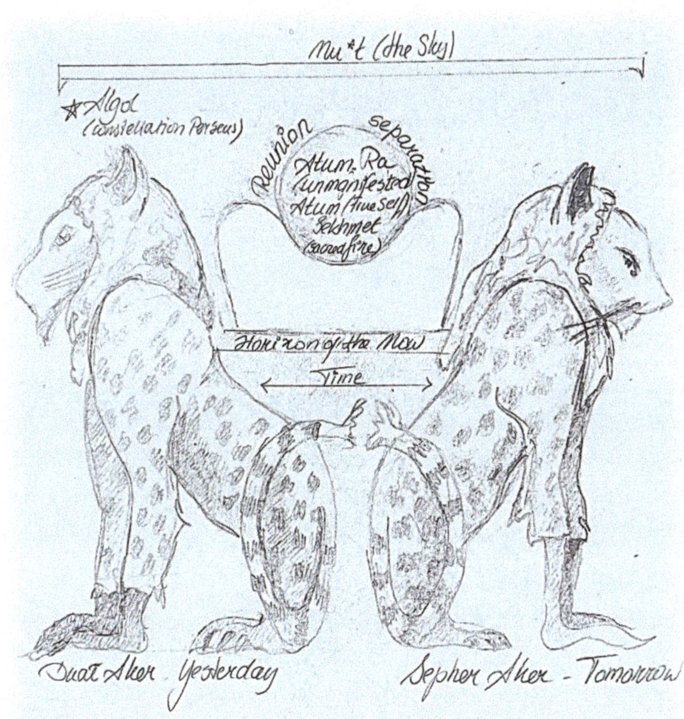

river. I observe the two jackals who guard the passage. The two animals are vigilant, their hair stands on end, and they face each other. The High Priestess declares that we have arrived at the shore of the Realm of Eternity, between the Tides of Time, between Yesterday and Tomorrow.

Hidden in plain sight, the Ocean Mother lies in the river. It is difficult to see her because she blends in completely with the landscape. Idris and I look at the back of her head, her hair floats on the flowing river Urness that streams from the Night to the Day – that lapis-lazuli-blue streaming beauty that reflects the flickering lights of torches and of the stars above. Her pregnant belly looks like a hill of dry land surrounded by water. Her legs merge with the Two Mountains of Sunrise and Sunset. I witness how the Ocean Mother gives birth to the Sun. Two midwives assist her in giving birth to the Sun; they form a part of the landscape as well; they are completely integrated into the Hills of Yesterday and Tomorrow.

The High Priestess is still in her place, backing towards the north, looking to the south. Behind her, the two priestesses raise their staffs, topped with moon symbols. Everyone is quiet now.

§ 75. The Birth of the Inner Sun

The High Priestess faces in the direction of the estuary where the river appears in the realm of the day above the ground. Everyone shifts their attention to the two hills at the exit from the Cave, which is guarded by the two jackals. The High Priestess lifts her arms, and again her mighty voice resonates over the landscape. Nature holds its breath in expectation of what is coming next.

Then I see the Waning Moon rising in the East, followed by the Morning Star Venus. I notice how the Ocean Mother's big pregnant belly swells even more. The two midwives step out of the shadows, and their silhouettes can be seen against the still dark sky. Above the belly of the Ocean Mother, the sky starts to turn blood red. The two jackals start to howl. Their shrill howl fills the air. The birds start to sing in chorus. The baboons wake up from their sleep, and they start to jump around, screech, and clap to welcome the newborn Sun. The waning moon climbs even higher, high above the horizon, at the place of Sunrise. The Sun follows the Moon and Venus, leaving the dark realms of the night, and starts to illuminate the Inner Earth.

Meanwhile, the sky turns purple, red, and pink. Idris tells me that all these reddish colors are the drops of blood the Ocean Mother sheds at the birth of the Sun. Together, this birth blood creates the Tree of Life. The Birth blood falls on the Earth and fertilizes the soil so that plants and animal life can be reborn after the winter season.

Then Idris points at the two jackals who guard the Gates of Life and Death. "*The names of these dogs are Wepwawet and Anpu. Wepwawet opens the Way to the realm of the Earth, that is the direction of the South, which is the Landing Place for all newborn life. Anpu opens the Way to the Fields of Offerings - this is the road into the realm of Eternity.*"

Then, over the edge of the belly, the sky starts to turn blood red. The two jackals howl, and we hear the voice of Eternity coming from the Deep:

I am the Creatrix of what comes into being.
I come into being in all the forms of Becoming
I am coming into being in Primordial Time

While I witness the Birth of the Inner Sun, I feel the *Flammae Sacerdotal* illuminating my entire inner being. My mind becomes illuminated from within. My vision of my life becomes embedded in a golden light. Everything I see, hear, touch, and feel becomes sacred. I see the sacredness of everything that surrounds me. Then I hear the voices of the priests and priestesses chanting at the same moment:

Blessed is the Giver of Life in her radiating beauty.
Blessed be her Wisdom and her Vision
Blessed is the Moon Road
that teaches us how to give birth to our Inner Sun
Blessed be her Child, Heru, the Inner Sun

The Force of Eternity pushes the Sun out of the Underworld, uphill. The Sun climbs, following the Moon Road. The Flood of Life follows the Sun after it is born. The Waters of the Urness stream downwards from the highest point of creation and flood the sowing fields of my Enchanted Lands, thus they also water my Magical Paradise Garden.

"This is the time to plant the golden seeds Eternity gave you at the beginning of your journey, Heru," Idris remarks.

I untie the knot from the pouch and remove it from the stick. I open the pouch and see how the seeds glitter in the light of the newborn Sun. I take them out. Then Idris comments: *"These are the talents that you will develop during the coming five years. What are their names and their qualities? Name them while you sow them in your Inner Garden."*

I do this, slowly and with concentration, as I sow them one by one in the freshly watered soil. Six golden seeds of the pomegranate, that have travelled with me through all the twelve caves. I name them one by one...

Then I hear Idris's voice again*: "My next question is: what do you take with you to the Hall of the Mountain King from this cave, Heru?"*

I bow my head and lay both my hands upon my heart. *"This feeling, my dear Idris, and the method by which I got it. The Moon Road is a powerful technique to enlighten the Inner Worlds. I take this method with me as a gift to the Wounded King."*

From above, a glittering shard whirls down and falls in front of my feet. *"Take the next shard from the Mirror of Heaven with you to the Round Table. This shard will complete the Golden Ring in the Hall of the Mountain King."*

Then Idris guides me back through the stained-glass door, and I return to the Hall of the Wounded King. When I step through the stained-glass door, the Hall is brightly illuminated. The King has risen from his bed and has taken a seat on the throne, at the head of the Round Table in the constellation Aries. In the center of the Hall, in the ceiling above the table, a stained-glass window is brightly lit by the Inner Sun.

§ 76. The Hidden Room

"Tap with your wand and lay one hand on the table," Idris instructs. I take my seat opposite the Wounded King, I tap my wand three times on the floor, and when I put both my hands on the table, a nebula starts to form in the infalling light, directly under the glass window in the ceiling. I look upwards. I see a six-pointed star appearing in the glass window. Then Idris encircles the entire room. With his wand, he points out the band of gold that encircles the entire hall, connecting all twelve stained-glass doors. Then Idris

speaks, his voice sounding completely different from before. Powerfully, his voice echoes through the entire Hall:

"Behold, the Golden Ring,
It is created from the Light of the Sun
When it travels around the Earth.
Because you have successfully made this journey,
You have earned your Magical Ring."

I hear the sound of an object falling. A golden ring falls in front of me. I pick it up. A text is engraved on the inside. It reads: *'Lapis Sancti Magi'*. I fit the ring, one by one, to my fingers. It fits perfectly on my forefinger.

"Heru, you have completed your first adventure, but your mission is not yet complete," Idris says, as he puts his right hand in his pouch and takes out a white cube. *"This is the Dice of Destiny, the Perfect Cube. It is a gift from the Goddess. Put it in your pouch with the rest of her gifts. This die is the symbol for your next quest: the Search for the Hidden Room."*

In the rays of light that fall through the ceiling, an object starts to materialize. A beautiful golden cup, covered by a veil, hovers above the Round Table. Idris continues: *"The central question on your next quest will be"*.

"What is the Grail, whom does it serve?"

Then a portal opens at the center of the hall and I get a vision: In a parallel world, I pass two white cypresses which stand at the entrance. A river enters into the Cave; it is the River Urness. At the entrance, a boat waits for me, which will carry me further along this magical river. I see that the boat passes through twelve caves. At the end of this journey, the river sails outwards and the stream goes forwards, upwards... straight into the night sky. The boat goes upwards on the stream of the River of Stars. Then I hear Idris's voice again:

"I ask access to the country called 'Exalted Bliss',
founded by the King called Total Vision.
Having no cushions on which to sit,
He has spread out the sea for a carpet.

Having no clothes to wear,
He wears the Mantle of Stars.
Having no food to eat, He feeds on the four elements.
Being jackal-eyed, he keeps away the dark both by day and by night.

His eyes are the Sun and the Moon,
and with his lights he reabsorbs everything that is not perfect.

I call upon the black and golden God
seated upon his dais
to lead me on my road over the Milky Way
into the realm of the sweet Perfumes of the Blue Lotus."

Then I see how the roof of the Hall fades, it appears to dissolve. I look directly into the night sky, and I see four great towers upholding the roof of an enormous Cathedral of Light.

The first tower is built from lapis lazuli blue stone. The building is topped with a statue of a Great Bull. On top of this tower burns a bright star, which radiates in all directions. It creates a beacon of light in the Eastern Hemisphere of Heaven. All the seekers who are on their search for the wisdom of the Ancient Sages are contacted by the light of the star Aldebaran, and are led in the direction of this temple. These are the Seekers for the fullness of life and the deep understanding of the Light.

The second tower is also made of lapis lazuli. This tower carries the image of an enormous Lion. Here, the Light of the Tower burns directly in the heart of the Lion. The Star Regulus makes a pathway for all of those seekers who search for the knowledge of the Star Temple, and walk the Path of the Light towards Integrity and the development of Spiritual Goals.

The third tower towers upwards against the deep blue night sky, and its lapis lazuli tiles are adorned with the image of a golden Scorpion. Here again, the light radiates to the most distant lands and creates the road leading to this temple. High above this tower circles an eagle. The light of this tower is the blood-red heart of the Scorpion – Antares. This is the Light that attracts the Seekers for Truth, Transformation, and the Connection to the Other Worlds.

The fourth tower is again a beautiful tower of lapis lazuli stones. Here we find the statue of Aquarius on the top. From the water basket of the Star Lord, the River Urness flows downwards from the highest heavens, creating a pathway of light. From the water basket jumps a fish, the spiritual essence of the star Fomalhaut. This star creates a pathway for the mystics and the magicians who are attracted by the pure beauty and harmony of the Work of the Spirit.

Then the vision disappears, and I am back at the Round Table. I reconnect with my body. I admire my Magical Ring and place the die in my pouch. In the distance, I hear singing...

House of Stars, adorned with Lapis Lazuli Blue
O Holy City, called Atlantis,
Founded upon a Dais in the Cosmic Oceans
Cathedral established for the rites of Magicians and Priests
House where the Incantations of Heaven and Earth are recited
Nothing evil can enter into this Holy Place
It is encircled and protected by a Veil of Light

Then the vision dissolves, and I find myself back at the Round Table in the Hall of the Mountain King. The Hall is abandoned. I contemplate my adventures in the silence of this magical hall. I feel the *Flammae Sacerdotal* burning bright, fulfilling me... but then the question pops up. Yes, I feel the Inner Light, it will illuminate my path into the future. But where will this path go? What is my goal? What is my personal mission? Then an urgent question comes to my mind:

"What is the Grail,
Whom does it serve,
And where do I find the Hidden Room..."

The King immediately responds. He sits upright in his bed, the Castle comes to life, the Hall fills with Lords and Ladies who prepare the hall for a great feast. While I see the changes in the Hall happening, I also notice that I am drawn back into my physical body. To my frustration, the Hall fades away, and with this last question in my mind, I sink into my physical body again. When I am fully awake and rise from my meditation seat, a swan feather falls before my feet...

The Golden Ring in Spring, Summer, Autumn and Winter

If you want to learn more about the myths belonging to the three Tarot cards of the winter season, visit the website. In the shop, you will find several video programs to deepen your knowledge even more.

https://www.hermeticartsandsciences.org/product/video-course-the-golden-ring-in-spring-tarot-journey-2/

https://www.hermeticartsandsciences.org/product/video-course-the-golden-ring-in-summer-tarot-journey-3/

https://www.hermeticartsandsciences.org/product/video-course-the-golden-ring-in-autumn-tarot-journey-4/

https://www.hermeticartsandsciences.org/product/video-course-the-golden-ring-in-winter-tarot-journey-5/

www.ingramcontent.com/pod-product-compliance
Lightning Source LLC
Chambersburg PA
CBHW061141220926
51851CB00008B/10
9789083585901